in association with  Brindleyplace

taste of birmingham
volume III

taste of
birmingham
volume III

First published 2006 by the Business Development Unit,
Weaman Street, Birmingham B4 6AT

ISBN-10: 0-9543388-5-5
ISBN-13: 978-0-9543388-5-5

Editor: Jon Perks
Design Editors: Darren Thomas, Oliver Shenton
Copy Editor: Narin Bahar
Product Manager: Anthony Bisseker
Photography: Craig Holmes
Production Manager: Julia Gregory

Printed by Butler & Tanner Group, Frome, Somerset

a **Trinity Mirror** business

Photography by Craig Holmes

Contents

All dishes are based on a serving of four, unless otherwise stated.

16 Al Faisals
Chicken desi masala

Chicken dilruba

Spicy lamb chops

26 Bar Estilo
Skewers of cod and chorizo with sweet potato mash

Grilled sardines with tomato and pine nut butter

Banana parfait

36 Birmingham Hippodrome Restaurant
Chicken and prune roulade

Baked fillet of lamb smothered with a chicken and mint mousse

Raspberry bavarois with ginger snap biscuit and peach coulis

46 Café Ikon
Chiperones rellenos

Higados de pollo

Crema Catalana

56 Chung Ying Garden
King prawn spring rolls

Fried fillet of beef in black pepper sauce

Fried mixed seafood with mange tout

66 cielo
Salad of roasted red peppers with Parma ham, olive crisps and basil

Cutlet of veal with Italian mushrooms, white truffle and Parmesan cream

Cappuccino of panna cotta, pomegranate and wild berries with biscotti

76 City Café
Egg Florentine

Sautéed fillet of turbot, creamed leeks, celery sauce, fennel tuille

Mint and dark chocolate soufflé

86 filini
Spaghetti and crab

Slow braised veal, white beans and creamed polenta

Filini tiramisu

96 Hotel du Vin
Dorset crab linguini with chilli, anchovy and caper butter, wilted pousse

Fillet of Scotch Beef Wellington, fondant potato, roast root vegetables, Madeira jus

Vanilla panna cotta with Champagne poached berries

106 Liaison
White crabmeat and Parmesan cappuccino with a crabmeat, ginger and coriander club sandwich

Roast squab pigeon with leg confit, blueberry and red onion tart, potato and apple fondant

White chocolate and mango cheesecake with a mango liquorice sorbet

116 The Living Room
Thai fishcakes, marinated cucumber with sweet chilli dip

Roast lamb cutlets with roast vegetables and mint pesto

Summer pudding

126 Malmaison
Onion soup gratinée

Roasted fillet of cod with Parma ham and vegetable broth

Chocolate fondue

136 The Oriental Bar Restaurant
Malaysian BBQ king prawns

Hot & sour pineapple cod – Nanas Assam cod

Malaysian spicy crab

146 Red Peppers
Goat's cheese and tarragon tarts

Fishcakes with mint and pea salad, lemon and herb mayonnaise

Chocolate parfait with fresh raspberries and cream

156 Simpsons
Salcombe crab cocktail

Sea bream with potato scales, creamed leeks, red wine sauce

Amaretti macaroon, poached cherries, Valrhona Ivoire chocolate sorbet, Morello cherry granite

166 Thai Edge
Tom Yum prawns

Lamb Penang

Thai sea bass

176 Turner's Grill
Leek salad with soft boiled egg

Belly of pork with black vinegar and char-grilled vegetables

Hot treacle tart with vanilla ice cream

186 House of Fraser Food Hall
Wines, Champagnes, deli delights, cheese, luxury chocolates and confectionery

197 Store cupboard and utensils

198 Cookery terms and methods

200 Glossary

200 Conversion tables

Foreword

This summer's Taste of Birmingham event perfectly captured just how far the city's restaurant scene has come in the last five years.

I saw at first hand just how warmly everyone embraced the four day food festival – from the restaurateurs who were there to cook their signature dishes to the thousands of people who came along to eat, drink and celebrate Birmingham's fabulous food offering.

It was absolutely phenomenal.

TV work and the likes of the BBC Good Food Show mean I have been a regular visitor to Birmingham over the last decade, so I have witnessed the dramatic transformation of not only the city and its dining scene but people's tastes.

The explosion of venues has been accompanied by an increase in awareness and knowledge of good food, as well as the people of Birmingham's ever discerning palates. Happily there is an increasing number of chefs and restaurants who can match these high expectations and demands.

Birmingham can now boast two Michelin star venues, along with many other high class restaurants offering a fantastic and diverse range of cuisine.

This book brings together a collection of many of these venues and their chefs, whose passion and professionalism shine through.

Whether the recipes here inspire you to try out some of the dishes in your own kitchen or simply draw you to visit the restaurants themselves, I hope you'll discover just what a great dining experience Birmingham has to offer.

Rese

Your table is ready…

taste of birmingham
volume III

Let your tastebuds guide you to Brindleyplace

The city of Birmingham is continuing to thrive as a truly cosmopolitan destination at the heart of England, with a growing reputation for international cuisine. And visitors to the city can experience a flavour of Birmingham's diverse food culture at Brindleyplace.

Known as the restaurant capital of Birmingham, this hugely popular waterfront location serves up a selection of 30 restaurants, cafés, bars and shops to cater for all tastes; with an exquisite choice of expertly produced dishes guaranteed to delight even the most discerning of palates.

A host of renowned establishments from Bank to Thai Edge and cielo to Café Rouge provide a choice of settings for Brindleyplace visitors, whether you want to enjoy a romantic meal for two or share a bottle of wine with friends. Many venues are family friendly and will happily accommodate your needs with dedicated children's menus available.

The bars and restaurants at Brindleyplace are complemented by the attractive tree-lined squares which characterise the area. A range of additional attractions including The National Sea Life Centre and The Crescent Theatre also combine to make Brindleyplace a hotspot among city workers and visitors to Birmingham.

Those who want to make the most of the immense choice on offer at Brindleyplace can take advantage of the Loyalty Card scheme. Loyalty Cardholders can save from 10 per cent off the price of a meal at participating restaurants, with

Ϸ Brindleyplace

Estate Management Office, 2 Brunswick Street, Brindleyplace, Birmingham B1 2JF
Tel: 0121 643 6866
www.brindleyplace.com

savings also to be made on other services at Brindleyplace. For that special occasion, the Brindleyplace Voucher Scheme means you can now treat someone special (or yourself) to an unforgettable experience at Brindleyplace.

The Brindleyplace Loyalty Card and Voucher Scheme can be redeemed against any participating retail, leisure or accommodation offering. They are accepted at The National Sea Life Centre, Crescent Theatre, LivingWell, Ikon Gallery and City Inn among others, offering something to appeal to all tastes.

For full listings of the restaurants, cafés, bars, shops, leisure and accommodation at Brindleyplace, visit the website on www.brindleyplace.com or drop into the Information Office and pick up a Guide.

 Brindleyplace

Estate Management Office, 2 Brunswick Street, Brindleyplace, Birmingham B1 2JF
Tel: 0121 643 6866
www.brindleyplace.com

Taste the world in one city

Fancy a taste of the Orient, indulging a passion for the Italian life or tantalising your tastebuds in Thailand? Then look no further than the city of Birmingham.

Lovers of international cuisine can leave their passports at home and forgo the nasty jabs in their search of global gastronomy.

Birmingham Bites, Marketing Birmingham's culinary campaign showcasing the city's diverse food and drink offering, aims to give food lovers a taste of the world all in one city.

More than 200 restaurants in the city centre enable food lovers to go on a global tour of Birmingham's diverse and exciting restaurant scene from Asia and the Americas to Europe and the Mediterranean.

For flavours of the east, visitors can head to Lasan on James Street, voted one of the top ten Indian restaurants in the UK, Itihaas on Fleet Street offering Royal Indian cuisine, Malaysian cuisine at The Oriental in The Mailbox and pan-Asian cuisine at Peppers on Bishopsgate Street – the first

Bollywood Champagne bar and restaurant outside London. Thai Edge in Brindleyplace and the new Kinnaree Restaurant in The Mailbox both serve traditional Thai dishes.

Chung Ying Garden on Thorp Street leaves Chinese food lovers spoilt for choice with 300 dishes. Wongs restaurant on Fleet Street regularly changes its menu to give diners a wide variety of fine dining cuisine.

Birmingham's two Michelin star restaurants, Simpsons and Jessica's in Edgbaston, lead the way in European fine dining; Andreas Antona, owner of Simpsons says: "Having been involved in the Birmingham restaurant scene since the early 1980's and being Governor of the Birmingham College of Food, Tourism and Creative Studies for over 10 years, it is great to see that Birmingham is now being seen as a food destination in its own right."

Fans of Japan can head for Wagamama noodle bar in the Bullring or to Shogun TeppanYaki in Brindleyplace for a more formal affair. For a taste of the Caribbean,

the Xaymaca Experience restaurant on Bristol Street is a real treat.

This international offering is also complemented by a host of people who have come from all over the world to hone their skills in Birmingham.

For an international flavour, head to the Jam House in St Paul's Square. This bar restaurant is the ideal place to combine a tasty meal with a great night out and has truly international connections in the shape of chef Kyawera Simpson who was born in Birmingham and brought up in Antigua. Having worked for Terence Conran in London, he is now back in his home city at one of the city's most exciting nightspots.

For more international cuisine and classy cocktails, Bar Epernay nestles alongside the 13 other bars and restaurants at The Mailbox. The bar serves classic tapas and delicious champagne cocktails and even comes complete with a revolving grand piano.

Hotel du Vin's Bistro on Church Street

Kinnaree

"Birmingham is now being seen as a food destination in its own right."

filini

also offers a menu rooted in classic European cuisine with a contemporary edge. Canadian Bruce Wallner is one of a kind as the first non-French sommelier working for the Hotel du Vin group.

Those who favour a truly cosmopolitan experience should try Aria Restaurant at the Hyatt Regency hotel which offers a varied menu that draws on Chinese, Japanese, Italian and Mexican influences. Harun Dursun, Assistant Food and Beverage Manager at the Hyatt adds an international flavour having relocated to the city in 2004 from the Hyatt hotel in Istanbul.

The filini Bar and Restaurant at the Radisson SAS Birmingham serves authentic Sardinian cuisine in contemporary surroundings. Head Chef Chris Duffy, who is at the forefront of the city's latest hotel restaurant, came to Birmingham from his home town of Glasgow where he also worked as a chef for the Radisson SAS hotel.

Cllr Mike Whitby, Leader, Birmingham City Council says: "Birmingham has a fantastic array of diverse restaurants and is becoming known as an international destination of choice. Visitors on the search for global cuisine can taste the world right here, a real treat for the tastebuds."

Alongside Birmingham's varied restaurants, foodies can also discover

delicious delis, food halls and food markets in order to browse and buy ingredients to create their own culinary delights.

Take your own tastebuds on a globetrotting delight using a Birmingham Bites Restaurant Map, now available in the city's TOA taxis and Tourist Information Centres located by the Rotunda and in New Street.

Peppers

birminghambites.com
TASTE THE WORLD IN ONE CITY

To unleash your tastebuds on Birmingham, restaurant listings and the latest foodie events, get your teeth into www.birminghambites.com or call 0870 225 0127 for visitor information about the city.

A new chapter for Taste

Birmingham's place on the culinary map was further strengthened in the summer of 2006 with the city's first ever Taste event.

Taste of Birmingham, which followed similar previous food festivals in London and Dublin, was held over four days in July and attracted over 18,000 visitors to sample dishes from the city's top restaurants, watch demonstrations and take part in wine and beer tasting classes.

Celebrity chefs Jean-Christophe Novelli, Aldo Zilli, Raymond Blanc and Antony Worrall Thompson performed in the Central Kitchen, whilst the likes of Roachford, Beverley Knight and Tony Christie entertained the crowds from the Heart FM Entertainment Stage.

Over 50,000 dishes were tasted, 10,000 glasses of wine drunk and 12,000 glasses of speciality beers downed during the event, which was presented by the Birmingham Mail and Birmingham Post and sponsored by Bank of Scotland Corporate.

Neil Rami, chief executive of Marketing Birmingham, said: "Taste of Birmingham was a fabulous event for the city and should be proud of its record breaking visitor numbers. The restaurants put on the best of their signature dishes for the

Taste of Birmingham

For the latest food news and information, visit
www.tasteofbirmingham.co.uk

Raymond Blanc entertains in the Central Kitchen

city, showing off the great range of culinary talent in Birmingham. We're already hungry for more!"

The festival also included the Taste of Birmingham Restaurant Awards hosted by Antony Worrall Thompson and ITV Central's Joanne Malin; celebrities including hairdresser Nicky Clarke, actor Johnny Briggs and Ruth Badger from The Apprentice presented a total of eight awards, including special recognition for Andreas Antona, owner of Simpsons, who was awarded an Outstanding Contribution to Good Food in Birmingham. Simpsons also won Best Restaurant of 2006.

Other winners on the night included Hotel du Vin (Best Wine List) and Bar Estilo (Best Family Venue).

For more information go to www.tasteofbirmingham.co.uk

"Taste of Birmingham was a fabulous event for the city and should be proud of its record breaking visitor numbers"

Taste of Birmingham

For the latest food news and information, visit
www.tasteofbirmingham.co.uk

Al Faisals

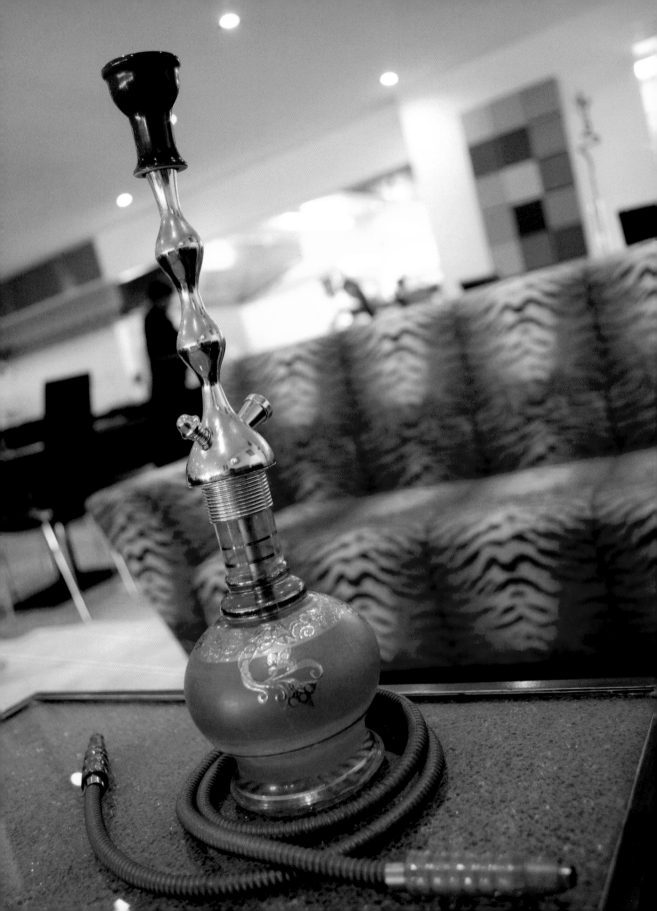

*Head Chef, Rohtash Kumar and
Restaurant Manager, Nitin Parasher*

Welcome to Al Faisals.

Located in the heart of Birmingham's Balti Triangle, Al Faisals stands out a mile. We offer a unique dining experience of Kashmiri Balti that is prepared in one of the oldest traditions of cooking and served in the most luxurious of contemporary settings.

Founded by Mr Ajaib Chaudhary more than 25 years ago, Al Faisals has developed and refined the art of Kashmiri cooking to near perfection. Our objectives are to maintain our high standards and traditional methods and to provide an efficient service in a warm and friendly manner.

Al Faisals re-opened to the public in July 2005 after undergoing a major refurbishment project and was named Best South Asian Restaurant of 2006. It is now one of the most lavish restaurants in the Midlands and has the food to match. We hope that all the investment we are making in Al Faisals will reward you with a positive dining experience worthy of your continued support.

Chicken desi masala

1/2 tsp salt

1/2 tsp turmeric powder

1/2 tsp red chilli powder

1/2 tsp coriander powder

20g ginger garlic paste

20ml oil

4 chicken legs

Method

Mix the salt, turmeric powder, red chilli powder, coriander and ginger garlic paste in with the oil.

Coat the chicken legs thoroughly in the mixture and then gently fry the legs in a heavy bottomed frying pan for 10 minutes until cooked through.

Serve with garlic coriander naan.

Al Faisals

136-140 Stoney Lane, Sparkbrook, Birmingham B12 8AQ
Tel: 0121 449 5695

Chicken dilruba

Serves 1

50g fresh dill, chopped

100g boneless chicken pieces

50g tomatoes, chopped

100g chopped onion

$^1/_2$ tsp ginger garlic paste

50ml cooking oil

$^1/_2$ tsp coriander powder

$^1/_2$ tsp cumin seed powder

Method

Firstly brown the chopped onion in a pan with a drop of oil. Put to one side.
Mix the oil, coriander powder, cumin seed powder and garlic paste together.
Warm in the bottom of a pan until the oil is hot and add the chicken chunks.
Coat them thoroughly with the spice and oil mix and stir fry for approximately
five minutes until the chicken is sealed.

Add the dill, chopped tomatoes and onion to the pan and stir. Simmer on
a low heat for 20 minutes.

Serve with pilau rice and naan.

Al Faisals

136-140 Stoney Lane, Sparkbrook, Birmingham B12 8AQ
Tel: 0121 449 5695

Spicy lamb chops

Serves 1

Ingredients

3 lamb chops

50g plain yoghurt

5g red chilli powder

5g garam masala

5g coriander powder

1 tsp salt

20ml cooking oil

Method

Stir the red chilli powder, garam masala, coriander powder and salt into the yoghurt until well mixed. Slowly add the cooking oil and stir through. Pour the marinade over the lamb chops, making sure to coat them thoroughly and then leave to settle for as long as possible – ideally a couple of hours so the meat can absorb the flavour of the spices.

Bake in an oven at 150°C for 20 minutes.

Al Faisals

136-140 Stoney Lane, Sparkbrook, Birmingham B12 8AQ
Tel: 0121 449 5695

Bar Estilo

Head Chef, James Killick

Bar Estilo is located in The Mailbox in a prime position next to the BBC and overlooking the canal.

Since opening in spring 2002 Bar Estilo has become a favourite place to meet, eat and drink for many city dwellers and visitors to Birmingham.

Our success is down to the wide choice of food and drinks on offer, coupled with a great atmosphere and friendly service; there really is something for everyone at Bar Estilo.

Those wishing to dine with us can either choose from a full à la carte menu or graze through a selection of dishes from our extensive tapas menu – a great way to dine with friends.

There's also a kid's menu with its own tapas selection which helped us to win Birmingham's Best Family Restaurant award in 2006. Bar Estilo is also a great place to stop for a drink whether it is a perfectly made mojito, one of our speciality sangrias or simply a glass of wine or beer.

We are open all day everyday, so call in after a hard day's shopping or pre-or-post theatre, and relax in style.

David Charalambous
Managing Director

Skewers of cod and chorizo with sweet potato mash

You will need 8 x 9" bamboo skewers, soaked in water

Ingredients

Cod and chorizo skewers:

1kg cod loins

4 cooking chorizo (approx 100g each)

2 small red peppers

2 small green peppers

1 large red onion

For the marinade:

60ml olive oil

2 limes (juice only)

1 tbsp coriander (finely chopped)

1 clove garlic (finely chopped)

$^1/_2$ tsp salt

$^1/_2$ tsp black pepper

Sweet potato mash:

650g sweet potatoes

650g mashing potatoes (eg Maris Piper)

30g butter

Salt and pepper

Method

Prepare the skewers:

Place the chorizo on a baking tray and cook in a hot (200°C) oven for 10-15 minutes. Remove from the juices and cool – reserve the juice. Cut the cod loins into even pieces (24 in total).

Cut each chorizo into 4 pieces.

Cut the peppers and onion into even sized squares (16 of each in total).

On each skewer alternatively place three pieces of cod and two pieces of chorizo with the peppers in between each one, and a piece of red onion at each end.

Mix all ingredients of the marinade together and pour over the skewers in a large dish.

Refrigerate for at least one hour.

Prepare the mash:

Peel the sweet potatoes and the potatoes. Cut into large pieces. Place in separate saucepans of cold salted water. Bring both to the boil and simmer until the potatoes are cooked. Drain and then mix the two in a large pot. Add the butter and mash together until smooth. Season with salt and pepper to taste.

Cook the skewers:

Oil a griddle pan and heat until smoking hot or preheat grill. Cook the skewers, turning on all sides until browned but not cooked through. Place in a baking tin and cover with the reserved chorizo juice and the marinade.

Place in a hot (200°C) oven for approx 6-8 minutes to cook through.

Serve immediately with the sweet mash and drizzle with the cooking juices.

NB
The cod can be substituted for other white fish such as monkfish.
It is important to cook the chorizo beforehand as it takes longer to cook than the cod.

Bar Estilo

110-114 Wharfside Street, The Mailbox, Birmingham B1 1RF
Tel: 0121 643 3443
www.barestilo.co.uk

Grilled sardines with tomato and pine nut butter

Ingredients

For the sardines:

8 sardines

Salt and pepper

Oil

For the tomato and pine nut butter:

125g butter

15g pine nuts

25g pitted black olives

25g semi-dried tomatoes

1 tbsp flat leaf parsley

Method

To make the butter:

Soften butter. Brown pine nuts in a dry frying pan over a low heat. Finely chop olives, tomatoes, parsley and toasted pine nuts. Mix into the butter and season with salt and pepper to taste. Refrigerate until needed.

Prepare the sardines:

Scrape off the scales from the sardines under cold running water. Remove the head and the guts and discard.

Season with salt and pepper and lightly oil. Cook under a preheated grill or in a griddle pan for a couple of minutes on either side until browned. Place in an ovenproof dish with a generous helping of the butter on each sardine.

Place in a hot (200°C) oven or back under the grill until the butter has melted and the sardines are cooked through.

To serve:

Carefully place on warmed plates and spoon over the butter.

Garnish with chopped flat leaf parsley and wedges of lemon.

Bar Estilo

110-114 Wharfside Street, The Mailbox, Birmingham B1 1RF

Tel: 0121 643 3443

www.barestilo.co.uk

Banana parfait

Ingredients

4 egg yolks

75ml water

70g caster sugar

4 egg whites

Pinch of salt

2 medium bananas

150ml double cream

100g ginger biscuits

35g butter

Method

Place the egg yolks, cold water and 50g of the caster sugar in a mixing bowl. Cook over a pan of simmering water, whisking continuously, on a low heat for approx 20 minutes until thickened.

Place egg whites and salt into a separate bowl and whisk until stiff, then whisk in the remaining sugar.

Peel bananas and blend in a mixer until smooth. Beat double cream until thick. Mix in the banana and double cream to the egg yolk mixture. Add the egg whites and combine all carefully together.

Smash the ginger biscuits into fine crumbs. Melt the butter and combine with the biscuits. Place the biscuit at the bottom of four individual mousse rings and press down firmly. Pour the banana mixture evenly over each base.

Freeze for at least 2 hours.

To serve:

Remove from freezer, gently rub the outside of the mousse rings with a warm damp cloth to loosen the parfait. Serve drizzled with toffee sauce or your favourite fruit coulis.

Bar Estilo

110-114 Wharfside Street, The Mailbox, Birmingham B1 1RF
Tel: 0121 643 3443
www.barestilo.co.uk

Birmingham Hippodrome Restaurant

Donald Deans, Head Chef

Next time you're planning a visit to Birmingham Hippodrome – whether for opera or ballet, a musical or family show, a comedy night or pantomime – come a little earlier, meet up with friends and relax over good food in stylish surroundings.

Browse through the evening's programme before taking your seats in the auditorium. Then return to your table for an interval drink, coffee or dessert.

Birmingham Hippodrome's popular restaurant, now managed by the theatre, overlooks the Hurst Street piazza and is the perfect meeting place for a pre-matinée lunch or early evening dinner and opens from two hours before curtain up.

A regularly changing à la carte menu and great value set menus are all available. And there's always a special offer for children. Our fresh popular dishes and extensive wine list, matched with attentive service in a relaxed atmosphere, will really make your next theatre visit complete.

Chicken and prune roulade

Ingredients

1kg minced chicken breast	150ml red jelly sauce (see below)
250g diced chicken breast	250ml each of brandy, port,
250g smoked back bacon	sherry
500g chicken livers	Seasoning
50g butter	Crispy leaf salad
75g diced prunes	
1 diced onion	Red jelly sauce:
2 cloves garlic	125ml port
50g chopped mixed herbs (coriander,	50g redcurrant jelly
tarragon, rosemary, sage)	2tbsps orange juice
1 egg yolk	2tbsps lemon juice
150ml chicken stock	Zest of $1/2$ an orange and lemon
4 slices of brioche	Pinch of English mustard

Method

Toss chicken liver quickly in butter in a frying pan over a fierce heat. Allow to cool for a few seconds, then place in a liquidiser.

Chop mixed herbs, dice onion and garlic and sweat off in a hot pan with butter.

Place port, brandy, and sherry in a pan over heat, and reduce by half. Leave to cool.

Make up 150ml of strong chicken stock.

Place minced chicken in a bowl. Add chicken liver mix, onion mix and liquor, and stock. Mix all together. Season with salt and pepper. Add egg yolk, continue to mix together.

Add diced chicken, check for seasoning and texture of mix. You should be able to spread this 'mousse' mixture like butter to bread.

Lay a sheet of tin foil onto the table, 15 inches long, then lay greaseproof paper on top of tin foil. Lay bacon on top of greaseproof paper, move in from the edges of the tin foil. The bacon should lay 10 inches long. Spread with mousse. Place chopped prunes along the centre and roll – it should be 3 inches in diameter. Seal both ends of the tin foil.

Place chicken roulade in a steamer tray and place in steamer for 45 minutes at 150°C; it should be probed to check it is 75°C.

Leave to cool, then slice.

To serve place two slices of the roulade in the centre of a plate, on a bed of crispy leaf, with toasted brioche and red jelly sauce.

For the red jelly sauce:
Blanch and refresh zest of orange and lemon.

Place all ingredients into a saucepan and bring to the boil; simmer to reduce by half.

Strain. Add zest of orange and lemon. Allow to cool before use.

Birmingham Hippodrome Restaurant

Birmingham Hippodrome, Hurst St, Birmingham B5 4TB
Tel: 0870 730 1234
www.birminghamhippodrome.com

Baked fillet of lamb smothered with a chicken and mint mousse

Ingredients

4 x 170g lamb fillets	Coriander	**Madeira sauce:**	Rosemary
85g chicken fillets	Fennel seeds	800g lamb bones	Thyme
2 jacket potatoes	1 red onion	2 onions cut in half	6 black peppercorns
28g chopped mint	1 aubergine	1 carrot	25g mushroom trimmings
Rosemary	1 courgette	1 stick of celery	50g redcurrant jelly
500ml chicken stock	28g red pepper	1/2 leek	125ml Madeira wine
28g butter	28g yellow pepper	1 whole garlic	300ml red wine
2 tbsps olive oil	28g green pepper	1 onion	
1 egg white	28g butternut squash	2 parsley stalks	
150ml double cream	2 cloves garlic	2 bay leaf	

Method

Remove excess fat from lamb fillets, season with salt and pepper and chopped rosemary. Place in fridge.

Place chicken in a liquidiser, add egg white, seasoning and cream to make a mousse. Pass mousse though a fine sieve. Add chopped mint. Place in fridge.

Wash and cut jacket potatoes into half; shape each half into large ovals. Place a little olive oil in a heated pan and lightly brown potatoes. Place and cover potatoes onto a roasting tray half filled with chicken stock. Add slices of butter to each potato and place in oven for 30 minutes at 150°C.

Prepare Mediterranean vegetables rough cut style. Place on a roasting tray and lightly sprinkle with olive oil, chopped coriander, fennel seeds and seasoning; place in oven to roast for 15 minutes at 150°C.

Remove lamb fillet and chicken mousse from fridge.

Place a little olive oil into a heated pan and seal fillets of lamb until lightly browned; remove from pan, place onto a tray and leave to cool.

Place chicken mousse into a piping bag with a star nozzle.

Pipe the mousse on top of lamb fillet. Place in a hot oven at 155°C for 8 minutes – mousse should be cooked through and lamb pink. Glaze under the grill.

To serve, place roast vegetables and fondant potato onto a plate, lamb on top of vegetables and serve with a Madeira sauce (see below).

For Madeira sauce (do a day in advance):
In a roasting tray roast lamb bones until brown.

Wash peel and roughly cut vegetables, brown in oven on a tray. Place tomato purée in a pan and heat for 3 minutes. Cut onion in half and brown on top of stove. Add red wine, bay leaf, rosemary, parsley stalks, thyme, mushroom trimmings, peppercorns, then the browned lamb bones, and browned vegetables to the pan.

Add enough water to cover and bring to the boil, skimming off any scum as it rises to the top. Simmer gently for 6-8 hours.

Make sure you skim off any fat if necessary. When cooked out strain into a clean pan and add redcurrant jelly, Madeira and seasoning.

Simmer, allowing the sauce to reduce by half, thickening the sauce and improving the flavour. Strain and serve.

Birmingham Hippodrome Restaurant

Birmingham Hippodrome, Hurst St, Birmingham B5 4TB
Tel: 0870 730 1234
www.birminghamhippodrome.com

Raspberry bavarois with ginger snap biscuit and peach coulis

Ingredients

For the bavarois:

180g milk

60g egg yolk

60g egg white

2 sheets gelatine

52g caster sugar

240g double cream

240g raspberries

4 x 3 inch sponge dishes

For the ginger snap biscuit:

135g butter

240g caster sugar

120g plain flour

120g golden syrup

4g ground ginger

Peach coulis:

2 fresh peaches (not canned)

300ml water

110g caster sugar

Juice of 1/2 lemon

2 bay leaves

Genoese sponge:

100g caster sugar

150g plain flour

100g butter

2 eggs

1/2tsp baking powder

Fruit syrup:

300ml water

100g caster sugar

Juice of 1/2 lemon

Juice of 1/2 orange

Method

For the bavarois:

Cream the egg yolk with the sugar. Boil the milk and whisk onto the egg yolk mix. Return to the heat and stir until it thickens (do not re-boil).

Remove from the heat and stir in the gelatine which has been soaked in 150ml of cold water for 3 minutes until it has dissolved. Strain and cool mixture until it reaches the consistency of half whipped cream. Wash and purée the raspberries, add to custard mixture.

Half whip the cream and fold into the custard mix you prepared earlier. Beat the egg whites and fold into the custard mixture. Line the base of a 3 inch mould with a thin layer of plain sponge (see right); brush with fruit syrup (see right). Fill the lightly greased moulds with the mousse and place in the fridge.

To serve turn out onto the centre of a plate, place ginger snap biscuit on top of bavarois with fresh raspberries; surround with peach coulis.

For the ginger snap biscuit:

Mix all the ingredients into a smooth paste. Roll out the paste and cut into equal sizes (called 'rounds'). Place onto a well greased tray, flatten them with your hand. Bake at 170°C until they are golden in colour. When cooked allow to cool slightly. Lift them off with a palette knife.

For the peach coulis:

Wash and peel peaches, cut into four, removing stones. Place in a pan with sugar, water, bay leaves and lemon juice. Bring to the boil gradually.

Simmer until peaches are soft. Remove from heat, leave to cool then liquidise. Pass though a sieve.

For the sponge:

Whisk the eggs and sugar with a balloon whisk in a bowl over a pan of hot water. Continue until the mixture is light, creamy, double in bulk. Remove from the heat and whisk until cold and thick (ribbon stage). Fold in the flour and baking powder very gently. Fold in the melted butter very gently. Place in a greased, floured baking tin.

Bake in a moderately hot oven (200°C for approx 30 minutes). Leave to cool and cut into the shape required.

For the fruit syrup:

Place all ingredients in a saucepan. Place onto the heat bring to the boil and simmer for 15 minutes.

Remove from the heat, strain into a clean bowl and place into the fridge.

Birmingham Hippodrome Restaurant

Birmingham Hippodrome, Hurst St, Birmingham B5 4TB
Tel: 0870 730 1234
www.birminghamhippodrome.com

Café Ikon

Chefs, Roy Bogle and Wesley Pinnock

In this our third entry to a Taste of Birmingham we are delighted to include some of our most popular tapas and puddings; recipes we are asked to divulge time and again.

As we approach our eighth year in our unique partnership with Ikon, I am pleased to say our relationship with this exemplary contemporary art gallery continues with gusto. Plans are afoot to extend our reception area, alter our furniture and increase the operating capacity of our kitchens, all designed to enhance the enjoyment of our loyal patrons and to extend the range and productivity of our contemporary Spanish menu.

Happily our core members of staff are still with us at Ikon and those who have returned to their native homes are regularly in touch. Our family and friends abroad have been most generous in hosting our visits to a variety of regions in Spain, France and Italy – indeed we have been guests at a couple of fabulous weddings – and look forward to some christenings soon!

As independent operators in an increasingly corporate world I am proud that we see so many of our friends return to Ikon, indeed they search us out in a city that is proud to move forward and change its face on what seems to be a daily basis. Long may 'Forward' be the city motto and long may we offer a slice of European hospitality.

To friends old and new muchos gracias y esperamos verle pronto.

James Marsden
Chef/Patron

Chiperones rellenos

Ingredients

400g fresh or frozen small squid (cleaned)

200g day old country bread – made into crumbs

2 cloves garlic – chopped

Handful of fresh chopped parsley

100g finely chopped Jamon Serrano – or other dry cured ham (optional)

100g raw prawns out of their shells – or other white fish

300ml sofrito, passata, or strained tomatoes

2 bay leaves

50ml dry sherry

80ml olive oil

1 lemon (juice only)

Method

To clean the squid; cut off the tentacles before the beak and eye and reserve, run the back of a knife along the body sack to remove and discard the skin, wings and a good deal of the internal sack.

Using a wooden spoon invert the body from the closed end and scrape out any further internal bits, especially the transparant "quill".

In a hot frying pan heat about 50-80 ml of olive oil, add the garlic – making sure not to burn and then add the breadcrumbs and ham, turn down the heat as the crumbs soak up the olive oil, the flavour of the ham and garlic and becomes crunchy. Add the chopped parsley add a touch of lemon juice and set aside to cool.

In a blender add the cooled crumb mix, the raw prawns and roughly blitz so all the ingredients are mixed together but not so the mixture is too puréed.

Stuff the squid bodies with the mixture to about half way and secure with a cocktail stick.

In a hot pan or griddle, brown the stuffed squid for about $1/2$-1 minute each side and remove to a serving dish. Gently warm the sofrito/passata, bay leaves and sherry to make a sauce. Cover the squid with the sauce – season to taste and bake in a moderate oven for 25-35 minutes.

The chiperones can be served hot or cold as a tapas or served with saffron rice.

The reserved tentacles can either be chopped into the stuffing mix or deep fried and used as an edible decoration on top of the squid – with some more prawns.

Café Ikon

1 Oozells Square, Brindleyplace, Birmingham B1 2HS
Tel: 0121 248 3226

Higados de pollo

Ingredients

400g fresh chicken livers (cleaned and patted dry)

50g butter

Splash of olive oil

Fresh sage leaves – chopped

50ml cream sherry

1 tsp icing sugar

2 tsps caperberries

150-200ml double cream

Fresh crusty bread – toasted with olive oil and sea salt

Method

Heat the oil in a pan until smoking – add the butter until it sizzles but does not brown. Throw in fresh chopped sage (about 6-8 leaves) and add the chicken livers to seal and brown both sides – be careful as they are liable to spit.

Dust with a teaspoon of icing sugar until just caramelised and deglaze pan with a small glass of sweet sherry.

Scrape the livers and bits from the bottom of the pan and add the double cream. The sauce should thicken and reduce. Add a little more of the cream if there is not enough sauce or a drop more sherry if it starts to split. Throw in a teaspoon or two of capers (washed whether they are salted or in vinegar) to taste and then pile on to the warm bread. Excellent as a tapas, a starter or, if very careful, a canapé.

Café Ikon

1 Oozells Square, Brindleyplace, Birmingham B1 2HS
Tel: 0121 248 3226

Crema Catalana

800ml double cream

1 tsp cardamom pods – crushed and
seeds removed

2 pieces of cinnamon bark – left whole

150g caster sugar

3 egg yolks

2 egg whites

80g caster sugar

In a heavy based saucepan add the cream, cinnamon, cardamom seeds and bring slowly to the boil then allow to simmer for up to 10 minutes to allow the aromatics to infuse.

In a clean mixing bowl whisk together the egg yolks and sugar to form a light paste then pour over the strained infused cream. In a double boiler, stir the custard until it is thick enough to coat the back of a wooden spoon. Reserve and allow to cool.

Whisk up the egg whites and gently combine into the cooled custard, transfer to cazuelas or ramekins and bake in a moderate oven (160°C) on a baking tin with enough hot water to come up to half way of the container (making sure none of the water goes into the custard). A good trick is to stand the custards on old newspaper in the baking tray and thoroughly soak this in boiling water.

After about 20-25 minutes the custards should be set, put to one side and allow to cool.

Cover the cool custard with the remaining caster sugar and caramelise either under a spanking hot grill or blow torch – and serve immediately.

Café Ikon

1 Oozells Square, Brindleyplace, Birmingham B1 2HS
Tel: 0121 248 3226

Chung Ying Garden

General Manager, James Wong

Chung Ying was established back in 1981 and was the first to introduce traditional Cantonese cuisine to Birmingham. It revolutionised how people ate their Chinese and quickly became a firm favourite with the locals. Chung Ying also transformed the local area to become what is now China Town. Having won countless of awards, Chung Ying Garden was set up in 1987, just a few yards away, to cope with the demand for this fashionable cuisine.

We have tried to keep the food as traditional as possible, typical of what you would get in Hong Kong (i.e Cantonese style), although each restaurant has its own style of cooking and head chef. Both restaurants are very popular amongst the local Chinese and have a special menu to cater for their taste.

Both restaurants has won countless of awards and recommendations, including awards from AA, Egon Ronay, Which? Good Food Guide and Harden.

Chung Ying Garden is one of the largest Cantonese restaurants in the Midlands, seating over 380 people and having four private dining rooms. We can cater for all types of events ranging from business meetings and seminars to corporate hospitality and private parties. We also have our in-house "Karaoke & Disco" which has proved very popular, especially over the Christmas period.

James Wong is the General Manager of the Chung Ying Garden and he has been working there for over eight years. He is the eldest son of the owner and effortlessly ensures to make sure the diners are well looked after. He is also the resident DJ over the weekend and also enjoys a sing-song!

King prawn spring rolls

Ingredients

1 clove of garlic	Pinch of salt and pepper
100g of king prawns	$1/2$ tsp of sesame oil
1 tsp potato flour	3 sheets of spring roll pastry
3 water chestnuts, finely chopped	$1/2$ tsp of cornflour
Pinch of sugar	Vegetable oil (for deep frying)

Method

Chop up the garlic into fine slices and deep fry. Leave on a kitchen towel to cool.

Wash and dry the king prawns.

Dice the king prawns and place into a mixer.

Add salt, pepper, sugar and potato flour into a mixer and slowly "blend" the mixture so that they are all stuck together. Make sure the prawns are not cut too fine.

Cut water chestnut finely.

Add the garlic, water chestnut and sesame oil to the mixture and use a spoon to mix. Add seasoning.

Get a sheet of spring roll pastry and cut in half.

Put the mixture into the pastry and then roll it up, sealing the sides (add a little cornflour with water and mix it into a paste... then use this as "glue")

Deep fry for 5 minutes on a medium heat.

Cut in half down the middle to check whether the prawn is cooked and then serve.

Chung Ying Garden

17 Thorp St, Birmingham B5 4AT
Tel: 0121 666 6622
www.chungying.co.uk

Fried fillet of beef in black pepper sauce

200g fillet steak	Pinch of salt
$1/2$ green pepper	Pinch of sugar
$1/2$ red pepper	1 tsp of dark soy sauce
$1/2$ onion	Clove of garlic
$1/2$ tsp ground black pepper	1 tsp cooking wine
$1/2$ tsp oyster sauce	300ml water
1 tsp of potato starch (or cornflour)	

Method

Slice the peppers and onion thinly.

Slice the steak thinly into manageable mouth-bite size.

Fry the steak lightly until "medium rare" and leave aside.

Heat the wok and add oil. When it is hot, add garlic and fry briefly.

Add peppers, onions, beef and black pepper and fry.

Add a teaspoon of cooking wine, 300ml of hot water, sugar, salt and oyster sauce and heat until boiled. Then take it off the heat.

Mix a little potato starch with water and add to thicken the sauce.

Mix a little dark soy sauce to colour and then serve with the beef.

Chung Ying Garden

17 Thorp St, Birmingham B5 4AT
Tel: 0121 666 6622
www.chungying.co.uk

Fried mixed seafood with mange tout

Ingredients

100g king prawns, cut half way through, to get rid of the "vine"	About 10 straw mushrooms, sliced in half
100g scallops, cut in half horizontally	1 tsp Chinese cooking wine
100g monkfish fillet, sliced	1 tsp potato starch (or cornflour)
50g mange tout	A pinch of salt
A little crushed ginger	$^1/_2$ tsp sugar

Method

Blanch the seafood in boiling water for about fifteen seconds (or when it boils) and drain.

Heat the wok and add oil.

Add garlic, ginger, mange tout, straw mushroom and seafood into the wok and then fried with a little cooking wine.

Take it off the heat and add a little salt and sugar to flavour.

Mix a little potato starch with water and add to the mixture to thicken sauce.

Put back to the heat and then serve when boil.

Chung Ying Garden

17 Thorp St, Birmingham B5 4AT
Tel: 0121 666 6622
www.chungying.co.uk

cielo

Executive Head Chef,
Andy Waters

cielo, regarded as one of Birmingham's finest Italian restaurants, can also boast a very exclusive address. Located at the prestigious and award-winning Brindleyplace development, cielo offers a complete dining experience, including al fresco dining overlooking the picturesque Oozells Square.

The recent appointment of Michelin-starred Andy Waters as Executive Head Chef underlines the quality of the food being served here.

The menu is classic Italian with a contemporary twist – whilst a fixed menu is available at lunchtimes and early evenings, when a children's menu is also on offer.

The interior combines pastel shades, chic furniture and a beautiful cascading water feature; music and lighting is adjusted to reflect the time of day and mood.

All of this, capped with the warm and friendly service, ensures a visit to cielo is a truly enjoyable and unforgettable affair.

Salad of roasted red peppers with Parma ham, olive crisps and basil

Ingredients

4 red peppers

2 cloves garlic – chopped

$^{1}/_{2}$ bunch basil

Olive oil – to drizzle

16 capers – dependent upon personal taste

16 pitted black olives – again, dependent upon personal taste

225g Parma ham – sliced

125g sun-dried tomatoes

$^{1}/_{2}$ ciabatta loaf – sliced

Method

Roast peppers in the oven until soft and then transfer to a bowl and cover the bowl with cling film – leave to cool.

When the peppers are cool remove the skin and seeds from the centre. Thinly slice the pepper skin and arrange onto your serving dish. Dress the peppers with chopped garlic, olive oil, basil leaves, salt and pepper, capers, black olives, Parma ham and sundried tomatoes.

Prepare olive crisps by thinly slicing ciabatta bread, sprinkle both sides with olive oil and then bake in the oven until golden brown. Garnish the pepper salad with the olive crisps.

cielo

6 Oozells Square, Brindleyplace, Birmingham B1 2JB
Tel: 0121 632 6882
www.cielobirmingham.com

Cutlet of veal with Italian mushrooms, white truffle and Parmesan cream

Serves 2

4 x 225g veal cutlets	**For the veal gravy:**
1/2 bunch fresh rosemary	1kg veal bones chopped small (ask your butcher)
225g assorted wild mushrooms	75g diced onion
150ml double cream	75g diced leek
75g Parmesan – grated	75g diced carrot
White truffle oil (to drizzle)	1/2 head of garlic
Oregano to garnish	50ml olive oil
Olive oil	5g thyme
	5g rosemary
	150g ripe tomatoes
	40g tomato purée
	700ml chicken stock
	200ml veal glace
	300ml water

Method

To make the gravy:

Roast the bones in a pre-heated oven (180°C) for 20-30 minutes.

Sweat the onion, leek, carrot and garlic in the olive oil, add thyme and rosemary, stir in the tomatoes and tomato purée and cook for 10 minutes

Transfer the roasted bones into a saucepan, add vegetables, veal glace, stock and 300ml water.

Bring to the boil and simmer for 30 minutes.

Pass through a colander and then through a fine sieve, finally pass through muslin.

To prepare the veal:

Marinade the veal cutlet in olive oil and fresh rosemary for 2 hours. Pan-fry the cutlet – when cooked remove and leave to rest.

To the pan add a selection of your choice of wild mushrooms and sauté, add gravy and reduce by half, season to taste and then pour over the veal.

Whip double cream until light and fluffy, then fold in the finely grated Parmesan cheese. Place a quenelle of the cream on top of the cutlet.

Garnish the dish with fresh oregano and white truffle oil.

cielo

6 Oozells Square, Brindleyplace, Birmingham B1 2JB
Tel: 0121 632 6882
www.cielobirmingham.com

Cappuccino of panna cotta, pomegranate and wild berries with biscotti

Ingredients

For the biscotti:

275g plain flour

150g golden caster sugar

1 tsp baking powder

1 egg yolk

2 whole eggs

1 tsp vanilla extract

110g whole blanched almonds

Icing sugar for dusting

For the panna cotta:

2$^1/_2$ sheets of leaf gelatine

4 tbsps milk

900ml single cream

1 vanilla pod

50g golden caster sugar

250g mixed berries of choice

300ml UHT milk

1 pomegranate

Method

To make the biscotti:

Heat oven to 180°C. Put the flour, sugar, baking powder, eggs, egg yolk, vanilla extract and almonds into a bowl. Mix together until a sticky, slightly soft dough is formed.

Tip dough onto a lightly floured board and knead for up to 5 minutes until it is smooth.

Lightly oil a baking sheet. Shape the dough into a log shape, put onto baking sheet. With a rolling pin, flatten the dough to a thickness of 2.5cm. Dust the top of the dough with flour. Score the dough at 2cm intervals, cutting two-thirds of the way down (makes approx 14 slices).

Bake for 20 minutes until pale golden colour and firm to the touch.

Cut through the markings whilst still warm, return to the oven for 10–15 minutes until golden colour.

Cool on a wire rack and dust with icing sugar.

To make the panna cotta:

Break the gelatine into a wide shallow bowl. Pour over the 4 tbsps milk and leave to stand for 5 minutes.

Pour the cream into a small pan. Split the vanilla pod and scrape the seeds into the cream, chop the pod and put into the cream, stir in the sugar, warm over a low heat, stir to dissolve the sugar until almost boiling, remove and discard the pieces of vanilla pod.

The gelatine will now look wrinkled and have soaked up most of the milk. Stir this into the cream until fully dissolved.

Cool slightly for 10 minutes and then pour into a serving dish.

Fill a third of a tall glass with the panna cotta mixture and leave to set. Fill the next third with a selection of seasonal berries.

Top with the cappuccino froth – heat and whisk UHT milk with a hand whisk and use the froth as your topping.

To garnish sprinkle with the pomegranate seeds.

Serve with a biscotti biscuit on the side.

cielo

6 Oozells Square, Brindleyplace, Birmingham B1 2JB
Tel: 0121 632 6882
www.cielobirmingham.com

City Café

Head Chef, Ian Boden

We opened City Café in March 2001. A quality, modern European restaurant in the heart of Brindleyplace. The restaurant, contemporary in design, is complemented by an all year round art exhibition. The recently refurbished terrace offers an extended season of alfresco dining.

Head Chef, Ian Boden joined City Café in April 2006, previously Head Chef of the French Restaurant at the De Vere Belfry as well as positions within some of the region's finest hotels – New Hall, Sutton Coldfield and the Birmingham Swallow. Ian's philosophy is simple wholesome, European food made with the highest quality and freshest ingredients and delivered at an excellent price.

Over the last year City Café has been developing its wine menu, sourcing quality wines from around the world working in partnership with Justerini and Brookes to ensure that we able to deliver exciting wines that complement our food.

Great food and wine build the foundations for an excellent experience; supported by attentive, professional service you are guaranteed a very memorable occasion.

Egg Florentine

Salt and pepper

100g spinach

12 eggs

1 block of puff pastry

50g Gruyère cheese

For the Hollandaise:

15ml white wine vinegar

5 egg yolks

250g unsalted butter

Method

Take your puff pastry and roll it out to ½ cm thick, cut out rounds, then use a cutter 2 sizes smaller in size than the one you have just used and score an inner ring on the pastry you have just cut out. Rest for 10 minutes then bake off at 180°C for 12-15 minutes.

When cold cut out the middle of the pastry using the scored mark.

For the Hollandaise:

Reduce the white wine vinegar by half, pour onto the yolks and whisk continually over a Bain-Marie of water. Meanwhile melt the butter in a separate pan. Once you get a good thick consistency, slowly add the butter a bit at a time. Store until ready to put the dish together.

Pan fry the spinach, poach the eggs in boiling water with a little white wine vinegar for 2 minutes then put two eggs in the pastry case, then top that with spinach. Then coat with the Hollandaise and Gruyère cheese and glaze under the grill.

City Café

City Inn Birmingham, 1 Brunswick Square, Brindleyplace, Birmingham B1 2HW
Tel: 0121 633 6300
www.citycafe.co.uk

Sautéed fillet of turbot, creamed leeks, celery sauce, fennel tuille

Ingredients

For each serving of turbot:

6oz fillet of turbot

10g unsalted butter

$^1/_2$ lemon, juiced

For each serving of leeks:

1 leek, sliced

50ml double cream, reduced by half

1 tsp chopped chives

For the celery sauce:

1 head of celery

50ml double cream

For the tuille mix:

100g flour

100g icing sugar

50g clarified butter

100g egg whites

Fennel seeds, toasted

Method

For the turbot:

In a hot non-stick pan place the seasoned turbot fillet presentation side down.

Sauté the turbot on the presentation side until half-cooked.

Add the butter and turn over the turbot.

Add the lemon juice and baste the turbot with the juices in the pan.

Remove the turbot and serve.

For the leeks:

In a thick bottomed pan, sweat down the leeks until tender.

Mix in the cream and the chives; serve.

For the celery sauce:

Using a juicer/liquidiser blitz the celery and extract the juices. In a thick bottomed pan reduce the celery juice by half.

Add the cream and bring to the boil. Remove from the heat and serve.

For the tuille mix:

Mix together the flour, butter, sugar and egg whites to form a smooth paste.

Using a stencil spread the mixture onto grease proof paper and sprinkle with the fennel seeds.

Cook at 160-170°C for 6 minutes until golden brown.

Leave to cool and serve.

City Café

City Inn Birmingham, 1 Brunswick Square, Brindleyplace, Birmingham B1 2HW
Tel: 0121 633 6300
www.citycafe.co.uk

Mint and dark chocolate soufflé

85g sugar

3 egg yolks

40g flour

225ml milk

75ml Crème de Menthe

30g dark chocolate drops

Butter and sugar, to line moulds

3 egg whites

First of all make the soufflé base; heat the milk and Crème de Menthe, until it starts to scald. Sift the flour. Beat the egg yolks, sugar and flour together, slowly pour the milk mix on the yolk mix whisking in at all times so the mix remains smooth. Pour back into the pan. Simmer gently, whisking at all times, for about 3-4 minutes until smooth and thick. Transfer into a clean container and chill for an hour.

To prepare the ramekin, melt butter down and using a pastry brush coat the inside of the dish with the butter, then fill the dish with sugar and empty it back out.

To make the soufflé, whisk the egg whites in a bowl, lightly fold them into the soufflé base along with the chocolate drops, spoon into the lined ramekins and place in the oven at 175ºC for about 11-12 minutes. Serve immediately.

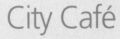

City Café

City Inn Birmingham, 1 Brunswick Square, Brindleyplace, Birmingham B1 2HW
Tel: 0121 633 6300
www.citycafe.co.uk

filini

Head Chef, Chris Duffy

As one of Birmingham's newest and most stylish restaurants, filini has proved a massive success with both diners and critics since it opened its doors at the Radisson SAS Hotel.

filini – meaning matchstick thin pasta – is an innovative philosophy in the world of food. The concept, designed by renowned restaurateur Roy Ackerman, is based on the simplicity and authenticity of beautiful dishes, offering an aromatic fusion that is the trademark of Italian and Sardinian cuisine.

Enviably located in the heart of Birmingham's city centre, within walking distance of the Bullring, The Mailbox and the theatre district, filini offers diners a varied menu, combining modern Italian dishes with a contemporary Sardinian twist. Fresh ingredients and an imaginative menu provide an exciting dining experience, whether you opt for a leisurely lunch or a decadent evening meal.

The restaurant reflects the hotel's fusion of modern and contemporary; walnut floors are reflected in convex mirrors on the walls and ceiling. The centrepiece of this striking restaurant is the amazing wine tower – an eye-catching glass structure made from weaved timber and metal plates. Lit and mirrored from the inside, the pineapple-shaped design can house 200 bottles of wine.

Spaghetti and crab

Serves 2

Ingredients

150g spinosi spaghetti	20g diced shallots
60g white crab meat	2g butter
10g diced tomato	Lemon oil
5g chopped chives	Olive oil
100ml fish stock	Sea salt
100ml white wine	White pepper
50ml double cream	

Method

In a small sauté pan, sweat down the shallots with a splash of olive oil.
Deglaze the pan with the white wine and reduce by half.

Add the fish stock and further reduce by half. Now add the cream and
reduce this by half again.

Once this is done remove from the heat.

Cook the spaghetti in salted boiling water and cook until soft then drain.

Add the spaghetti to the sauce and return to heat. Once the sauce starts to
boil take off the heat then fold in the butter. Add the crab, tomato and chives
and warm through.

To finish season to taste with sea salt, pepper and a drizzle of lemon oil.

filini

Radisson SAS Hotel, Holloway Circus, Queensway, Birmingham B1 1BT
Tel: 0121 654 6000

Slow braised veal, white beans and creamed polenta

Serves 6

For the braised veal:

12 veal cheeks

250g finely diced carrots

250g finely diced celery

6 peeled button onions

250g finely diced leek

200g finely chopped shallots

3 garlic cloves

Bunch of thyme

Small bunch of tarragon

Small bunch of oregano, chopped

1 bay leaf

1.5l veal stock

1 bottle Barolo wine

3 plum tomatoes (peeled and 10mm diced)

120g Figioli beans, cooked in stock

For the polenta:

125g polenta flour

1.2l milk

100g Parmesan

20g butter

Sea salt and pepper

Method

For the braised veal:

In a deep heavy pan seal off the veal cheeks, add the carrots, celery, garlic, shallots, button onions and leeks and caramelise. Deglaze the pan with the Barolo wine and reduce by half.

Add the veal stock and bring to the boil, throw in the bay leaf, thyme and tarragon, turn down the heat and let simmer with a lid on for about 2 hours.

Take off the lid for the remainder of cooking so to let the stock reduce by about half. Just before you take off the heat add the beans, diced tomato and oregano and season to taste.

For the polenta:

Put the polenta into a large jug so it can be poured in at a steady stream. Bring the milk to the boil in a large heavy saucepan; add a teaspoon of salt and add in the polenta at a slow steady rate, whisking all the time until completely blended. Take the polenta off the heat and add the butter and Parmesan at the same time, whisking to a smooth paste.

filini

Radisson SAS Hotel, Holloway Circus, Queensway, Birmingham B1 1BT
Tel: 0121 654 6000

filini tiramisu

Serves 2

4 eggs, separated

100g caster sugar

500g Mascarpone cheese

6 tbsps Marsala wine

250ml fresh black coffee

16 Savoiardi biscuits

2 tbsps sugar

Finely grated chocolate

Beat the egg yolks and 100g of the caster sugar together over a light heat until pale and stiff. Add the mascarpone and beat until smooth.

Whisk in the Marsala. Place in fridge. In a clean bowl, whisk the egg whites and 2 tablespoons of sugar until stiff, then fold in the Mascarpone mixture. Return to the fridge for 30 minutes. Put the black coffee in a bowl, briefly soak the biscuits in it, then set aside.

Fill the glass with alternate layers of cream and biscuit. To finish dust with grated chocolate. Garnish with mint, orange slice and biscuits as shown.

filini

Radisson SAS Hotel, Holloway Circus, Queensway, Birmingham B1 1BT
Tel: 0121 654 6000

Hotel du Vin & Bistro

Head Chef, Nick Turner

Here you will find 'simple classics' that change seasonally, with Head Chef Nick Turner adding his own selections daily, all supporting our philosophy of using the finest and freshest local produce, cooked simply, priced sensibly.

An extensive and eclectic wine list is a key feature of the hotel. In addition to the main list, which includes an impressive array by the glass, there is a small daily selection of good value wines to complement the menu. Head sommelier François Bourde and his team are always happy to give friendly, knowledgeable advice.

Dorset crab linguini with chilli, anchovy and caper butter, wilted pousse

Ingredients

For the pasta:

600g plain white flour

4 eggs

6 egg yolks

300g white claw crab meat

2 tbsps olive oil

A pinch of salt

Handful of pousse (a type of spinach)

For the chilli butter:

150g butter (unsalted)

2 red chillies

1 chopped shallot

2 tbsps fine capers

Sprig of dill

Sprig of flat parsley

Juice and zest of a lemon

4 anchovy fillets

Seasoning

Method

For the pasta:

Place flour in a food processor and switch on, add the eggs and egg yolks, slowly using the pulse button.

Add the olive oil and salt, remove from machine and knead for a few minutes and rest wrapped in cling film for 1 hour.

For the butter:

Finely chop shallot and deseeded chilli, place in a bowl with softened butter, chopped herbs, lemon juice and zest, capers and chopped anchovies.

Season and mix together, roll into sausage in cling film and refrigerate.

To serve:

Roll out pasta on pasta machine and cut into linguini, blanch in boiling water with a little oil.

Pick crab meat to check for shell and place in a pan with a knob of chilli butter and the pasta that has been cooked and drained. Toss together, with a little pousse.

Arrange on plate and drizzle over a little olive oil and serve.

Hotel du Vin & Bistro

25 Church Street, Birmingham B3 2NR
Tel: 0121 200 0600

Fillet of Scotch Beef Wellington, fondant potato, roast root vegetables, Madeira jus

Serves 2

Beef Wellington:

350g centre cut Scotch beef fillet
80g mushroom duxcelle
300g puff pastry
1 egg yolk
1 herb pancake (see right)
100ml olive oil
Seasoning

Fondant potato:

2 large baking potatoes
50g butter
500ml stock (vegetable or chicken)

For the mushroom duxcelle:

140g finely chopped button mushrooms
2 finely chopped shallots
30g butter
Seasoning

Roast root vegetables:

1 large carrot
1 swede
Knob butter
1 tbsp honey

Madeira jus:

200g beef trimmings
1 shallot
1 clove garlic
Sprig of thyme
250ml red wine
30ml Madeira
300ml veal stock

Herb pancake:

100g plain flour
1 egg
300ml milk
Pinch of freshly chopped chervil, parsley and chives
Pinch of salt
100ml vegetable oil

Method

For the Beef Wellington:

Roll out puff pastry until 4mm thick, refrigerate and relax. Heat oil and season beef, seal until golden brown on all sides. Cool.

Make pattie with duxcelle (see right) and place on top of beef like a crust, cover with pancake (see right) and then wrap over puff pastry. Egg wash edges and tuck under forming a parcel and egg wash over.

To cook place on baking tray in a pre-heated oven at 180°C for 25-30 minutes, leave to rest for 5 minutes.

For the fondant potatoes:

Cut potatoes out with a cutter into a cylinder shape and trim edges with a peeler.

Spread butter on bottom of pan and place in potatoes (trimmed edges faced down) and cover half of the potato with stock.

Cover with greaseproof paper and cook until potato is soft, then remove greaseproof and caramelise butter, leave to cool and remove from pan.

For the mushroom duxcelle:

Melt butter, soften shallots and add mushrooms, cook slowly until all water has evaporated, season and cool.

For the roast root vegetables:

Turn carrot and swede into barrel shapes, cook in boiling water for two minutes and dry.

Heat butter until nut brown, add carrots and swede, finish with a little honey and brown.

For the Madeira jus:

Brown beef trimmings, add shallot, garlic and thyme. Add wine and reduce until syrupy, add stock and reduce by half. Finish by adding the Madeira. Reduce until required consistency and season.

For the herb pancake:

Place the flour and salt in a food processor and add the egg and half of the milk. Blend until smooth. Add the rest of the milk. Leave to stand for 20 minutes and stir in the chopped herbs.

Cook in a non-stick pan with a little oil until golden brown and leave to cool on a cooling rack.

Hotel du Vin & Bistro

25 Church Street, Birmingham B3 2NR
Tel: 0121 200 0600

Vanilla panna cotta with Champagne poached berries

For the panna cotta:

125ml milk

375ml double cream

50g caster sugar

1 lemon zest

1 vanilla pod

2 gelatine leaves

For the berries:

1 punnet raspberries

1 punnet strawberries (other berries can be added)

400g sugar

1 vanilla pod

200ml water

$^{1}/_{2}$ bottle Champagne

For the panna cotta:

Place all ingredients except gelatine into a pan and bring to the boil.

Soak gelatine in a little water until soft and then stir into the rest of the ingredients, pass through sieve and pour into small pudding moulds and refrigerate.

For the berries:

Heat Champagne, water, vanilla pod and sugar until boiling, pour over washed berries and leave to cool.

To serve:

Run a little warm water over the base of the pudding mould to release the panna cotta, place in the middle of a plate and arrange the berries around.

Hotel du Vin & Bistro

25 Church St, Birmingham B3 2NR
Tel: 0121 200 0600

Liaison Restaurant

Chef Patron, Patricia Plunkett

Liaison Restaurant is a cherished haven for discerning diners.

Conveniently situated on the A34, Stratford Road, at the border of Solihull and Hall Green, its stylish and elegant décor exudes restrained luxury and refined taste.

Here is a refuge from the hustle and bustle of every day life where you can enjoy inspired dishes. It is ideally placed for visitors to Birmingham, the National Exhibition Centre, Stratford-Upon-Avon and has built up a considerable following of local residents.

Patricia Plunkett and Ank van der Tuin opened the original Liaison 25 years ago in Solihull and their restaurants have been exciting diners with their imaginative food ever since. Using a wide variety of subtle flavours and textures the dishes are presented in Liaison's signature contemporary style. Having once sampled the food, diners return time after time.

The dishes, which blend tradition and innovation, are created by the Liaison's exciting and enthusiastic young team under the experienced guidance of Chef Patron, Patricia Plunkett.

Ank and Trish invite you to try the Liaison experience.

White crabmeat and Parmesan cappuccino with a crabmeat, ginger and coriander club sandwich

Ingredients

Parmesan crisps:

100g grated Parmesan

Cayenne pepper

Crabmeat cappuccino:

200g white crabmeat

150ml single cream

125ml fish stock

Pinch cayenne pepper

Salt and pepper

1 tbsp finely grated Parmesan

25ml Noilly Prat

1 leek

1 onion

2 sticks celery

10g butter

Club sandwich:

200g white crabmeat

2 tbsps good quality mayonnaise

6 sprigs coriander finely chopped

$\frac{1}{2}$ lime freshly squeezed

1 tbsp ginger preserve

1 brioche loaf

Method

Club sandwich:

Slice brioche thinly and cut into rectangle shapes. Toast in oven until lightly brown. Mix all other ingredients together and spread on toasted brioche, finish by spreading top brioche slice with mayonnaise and sprinkle with chopped coriander.

Crabmeat cappucino:

Dice vegetables and cook in butter until soft, deglaze with Noilly Prat, add fish stock, bring to boil then simmer for 15 minutes. Blend and pass through sieve. Add cream, crabmeat, Parmesan and seasoning.

Heat gently and serve topped with Parmesan crisp.

Parmesan crisps:

Line baking sheet with parchment paper. Shape Parmesan into small rectangles (2cm by 10cm) and sprinkle cayenne on top. Cook in oven at 165°C until soft and golden. Allow to cool and store between parchment paper until needed.

Liaison Restaurant

1558 Stratford Road, Hall Green, Birmingham B28 9HA
Tel: 0121 733 7336
www.liaisonrestaurant.co.uk

Roast squab pigeon with leg confit, blueberry and red onion tart, potato and apple fondant

Serves 2

| 2 squab pigeons |
| 25g blackcurrant vinegar |
| 125ml red wine |
| 50g Crème de Cassis |
| 1 onion, carrot and leek (for stock) |
| 1 small tin duck fat |

Potato and apple fondant:

| 4 medium potatoes (King Edwards preferable) |
| 400ml chicken stock |
| 100g butter |
| Salt and pepper |
| 75g good quality apple sauce |
| 100ml double cream (to be whipped) |

Red onion and blueberry tart:

| 100g puff pastry |
| 75g blueberry jam |
| 1 medium red onion |
| 10ml blackcurrant vinegar |
| 30g brown sugar |
| Small punnet blueberries |

Method

Squab pigeon:

Remove breasts and legs from pigeons, leaving wing bone on the breast. Confit the pigeon legs in melted duck fat in low oven until tender (approx 1 hour).

For stock, roast pigeon bones and vegetables together until brown, transfer to saucepan and cover with water, deglaze roasting pan with vinegar and red wine, add to stockpot and simmer for 45 minutes.

Strain, add Crème de Cassis, taste for seasoning. This is your sauce.

Fry pigeon breasts on high heat until golden. Transfer to hot oven (190ºC) for 8-10 minutes.

Slice pigeon breast and serve with leg confit, blueberry tart and fondant; coat with sauce.

Potato and apple fondant:

Peel potatoes, cut into cylinder shapes and place in small baking dish. Pour over stock, place small knob of butter on each potato, season and cook in oven 170ºC for 40 minutes.

Allow to cool. Using an apple corer take centre out of potato. Make apple mousse by folding apple sauce into whipped cream. Before serving heat potato, pipe apple mousse into centre and blow torch (or grill at high heat) to caramelise.

Red onion and blueberry tart:

Sweat diced onion until soft, add vinegar, sugar and blueberry jam. Stir until completely mixed. Remove from heat and add fresh blueberries. Roll out puff pastry and cut into 4 inches circles. Shape into a muffin tray, bake at 170ºC for 12-15 minutes until brown.

Fill with blueberry mixture and cook in oven for a further 5 minutes.

Liaison Restaurant

1558 Stratford Road, Hall Green, Birmingham B28 9HA
Tel: 0121 733 7336
www.liaisonrestaurant.co.uk

White chocolate and mango cheesecake with a mango liquorice sorbet

This recipe requires an ice cream maker
Serves 2

Ingredients

For the cheesecake filling:

500g good quality white chocolate

500ml double cream

50ml Malibu

Juice and zest of 1 lime

400g cream cheese

Mango liquorice sorbet:

1 large mango, peeled and puréed

200ml water

100g sugar

20g liquid glucose (available from most pharmacists)

75g mango liquorice, finely diced

Spiced ginger base:

1 small pkt digestive biscuits

10g ground ginger

10g cinnamon

50g demerera sugar

100g melted butter

Method

Cheesecake filling:
Melt white chocolate, whip cream, fold both together, then add lime juice, zest, Malibu and cream cheese and mix until smooth consistency. Pour into prepared biscuit base and chill until set.

Spiced ginger biscuit base:
Blend biscuit in a food processor with the spices and sugar until they resemble crumbs, bind together with melted butter. Press crumbs into a small rectangular baking dish, pour cheesecake mixture on top and refrigerate until set.

Sorbet:
Put water, sugar and glucose into a heavy base saucepan, bring to boil, simmer for 5 minutes. Allow to cool, blend with mango flesh, strain and churn in an ice-cream maker until sorbet consistency. Add diced liquorice and churn for a further 5 minutes. Freeze until ready to serve.

Liaison Restaurant

1558 Stratford Road, Hall Green, Birmingham B28 9HA
Tel: 0121 733 7336
www.liaisonrestaurant.co.uk

The Living Room

Head Chef, Dan Ribton

As The Living Room proudly approaches its seventh year of success, this iconic venue has grown in both stature and presence. Boasting a mature attitude towards dining and socialising, The Living Room has remained incredibly popular through imagination and continual reinvention; whilst it has kept at its heart the core of its offering – good food and drink, prepared simply and served impeccably.

Influences are eclectic, yet the focus remains on two broad types of cuisine; a section of 'Home Comforts' honours that long loved gastro pub flavour.

Dishes to satisfy an honest appetite for wholesome hearty cooking, served always with an enviably quirky 'Living Room' twist. The second style suits the more refined pallet, an elegant European/global fusion interspersed with fine British Classics. If food were music, this menu would certainly be Jazz! These dishes will make an impression and are certain to impress, yet the theory behind them is simple; fresh ingredients expertly infused with flavours known, loved and trusted.

The eating experience is of paramount importance to The Living Room. Every detail has been considered to create an effortlessly ambient environment; airy, open and drenched in natural daylight – yet simultaneously intimate and cosy. Each evening, live music resounds from the legendary baby white piano animating the restaurant and creating a dining sensation that has inspired guests to return and to consider the venue a true home from home.

Thai fishcakes, marinated cucumber with sweet chilli dip

Serves 6
You will need a deep fat fryer

Ingredients

Fishcakes:

500g fresh salmon (bones & skin removed)

1 egg white

2 tsps wasabi (Japanese horseradish, ready made)

4 spring onion, sliced very thinly

25g fresh coriander, roughly chopped

3 slices white bread

200g potato

2 dsps tom yum paste

1 tsp salt

Black milled pepper

4 cloves garlic, peeled, crushed then finely chopped

1 tsp chilli flakes

2 dsps ginger – peeled then finely grated

Marinated cucumber:

1 whole cucumber

1 lemon

5 dsps soy sauce

5 dsps rice vinegar

5 dsps sesame oil

2 dsps demerara sugar

Pinch of chilli flakes

To serve:

3 limes (cut in half on slight angle)

18 dsps sweet chilli sauce

Method

For the fishcakes:

Place half of the fresh salmon and the egg white into a food processor and pulse until the fish is broken up; you want the fish to still have some texture and not be blended smooth. Place into a mixing bowl.

With the rest of the salmon chop into small dice and place into the bowl. Place the bowl into the fridge and keep until needed.

Place the peeled potatoes into cold salted water and bring to the boil, cook for approximately 10 minutes. Drain and air dry for about 5 minutes then mash until there are no large lumps.

Ensure that the crusts are removed from the sliced bread then pulse in the food processor to form loose fresh white breadcrumbs.

Place all the rest of the ingredients (breadcrumbs, potato, wasabi, coriander, spring onion and seasoning etc) into the mixing bowl with the salmon you prepared earlier. Gently fold the mix together, do not over work as you want all the ingredients to hold their form.

Place the mix into the fridge and allow to set up for approximately 15 minutes. Split the mix into 18 equal size balls then flatten into 1cm thick cakes; place onto silicon paper and refrigerate until needed.

Pre-set a deep fat fryer to 180ºC.

Deep fry the cakes until golden and piping hot in the centre, this should take no longer than 2 minutes.

Equally split the marinated cucumber between the six plates, arrange the cakes on top of the cucumber and serve the lime wedges and sweet chilli sauce on the side.

To make the marinated cucumber:

Place the grated zest of lemon into the mixing bowl, squeeze the lemon juice and remove the pips.

Add the sugar and place into the microwave and gently heat the juice until the sugar dissolves.

Add the soy sauce, rice vinegar, sesame oil, chilli flakes and mix thoroughly. Allow to cool.

Shred the cucumber with a mandolin (if you do not have one, use a grater) into long thin strips, add to the mixing bowl and toss together.

Only marinate the cucumber for a maximum of 10 minutes.

The Living Room

Unit 4, Regency Wharf, 2 Broad St, Birmingham B1 2JZ
Tel: 0870 4422539
www.thelivingroom.co.uk

Roast lamb cutlets with roast vegetables and mint pesto

Serves 6

Ingredients

Mint pesto:

5 dsps roasted pine nuts

5 cloves roasted garlic

25g fresh mint

7 dsps olive oil

1 dsp mint sauce

Black milled pepper

Pinch salt

Roast vegetables:

1½ red peppers

1½ yellow peppers

1 whole aubergine

3 small courgettes

1 medium red onion

100ml olive oil

Salt

Pepper

For the lamb cutlets:

18 x 65g lamb cutlets (French trimmed)

Extra virgin olive oil

Salt

Freshly milled pepper

Method

To make the pesto:

Place the fresh garlic in its skin into an ovenproof dish and drizzle with a little olive oil and season with salt and pepper, place into a medium oven approx 180°C and roast for approximately 10 minutes until the garlic is soft and golden.

Place the fresh mint (stalks and leaves) into a liquidiser, add half of the olive oil and blend until the mint is completely blended smooth, add the rest of the olive oil during the blending.

Place the blended mint and olive oil into a mixing bowl, add the mint sauce and stir together.

Crush the roasted pine nuts so that they become broken up, add them to the mixing bowl. Pop the roasted garlic from its skin then slice each clove into 3 or 4 slices then add to the bowl.

Mix all the ingredients together thoroughly and taste, if it requires more seasoning then add to your taste.

Place into a suitable container and keep in the fridge until needed.

To prepare the vegetables:

Trim the stalk from the peppers but leave on the heart of the stem. Cut each pepper in half, then each half in half to give 4 quarters per pepper. Heat a char-grill pan until almost smoking. Lightly oil and season the pepper quarters, drain off any excess oil and using extreme care place the peppers skin side down into the pan.Cook for approximately 3 to 4 minutes depending on the heat of the pan; turn the peppers over and cook on the over side for the same amount of time (the peppers need to have a charred outside but without being burnt).

Cut the aubergine into 12 x 1cm thick rounds, add a little salt and place into a colander and leave for 30 minutes. Once the

aubergines are drained, pat dry with some kitchen cloth, and grill in the griddle pan, this will only take 1 to 2 minutes per side, turning the rounds 90 degrees to give a criss cross effect on both sides.

Place onto a tray and allow to cool.

Slice the courgettes into long ½cm thick ribbons – you should get about 4 per courgette.

Place the courgettes into the pan and repeat as for the aubergine, once marked place onto the tray and season with salt and pepper and drizzle with some olive oil.

Slice the red onion into ½cm thick rounds, leaving the skin on to keep the slices together; lightly oil and season, again cook in the griddle pan. Cook for approximately 3 to 4 minutes per side or until the onions are caramelised on both sides, once cooked place onto the tray and reserve until needed.

For the lamb cutlets:

Place the lamb cutlets onto a tray and lightly season with salt and pepper, lightly oil on all sides.

Place the roasted vegetables into an oven proof dish, place into a medium oven – you only need to get the vegetables hot as they are already cooked, this should take no longer than 6 to 8 minutes.

Ensure that the griddle pan is very hot, place the cutlets into the pan and cook for 4 to 5 minutes per side, then remove from the pan and place onto a tray and allow to rest for 3 minutes (keeping them warm). The lamb needs to rest otherwise it may be tough to eat. If you require your lamb more cooked than 'pink' (ie medium) then cook for a further 2 to 3 minutes per side.

Once the lamb cutlets are rested and the vegetables are very hot, serve as desired. Garnish with the mint pesto and drizzle the vegetables and lamb with the extra virgin olive oil.

The Living Room

Unit 4, Regency Wharf, 2 Broad St, Birmingham B1 2JZ

Tel: 0870 4422539

www.thelivingroom.co.uk

Summer pudding

Serves 6

2 punnets raspberries

2 punnets strawberries

1 punnet blackberries

1 punnet blueberries

1 loaf, thin sliced white bread

50g unsalted butter

For the raspberry purée:

500g frozen raspberries (defrosted)

50g caster sugar

Stock syrup:

300ml water

375g caster sugar

To decorate:

Mint sprigs

Icing sugar

300ml double cream

To make the purée, blend the defrosted raspberries and sugar to form a smooth purée, then pass through a fine sieve. To make the syrup, place the water and the 375g of sugar into a pan and bring to the boil, boil for at least 4 to 5 minutes, remove from the heat and allow to cool.

Mix together the stock syrup and half of the raspberry purée thoroughly.

Bring to the boil, add the washed berries, then reduce to a simmer for 1 minute, then remove from the heat and allow to cool.

Lightly butter the inside of six dariole moulds (see glossary). The fruits will start to soften but not lose their shape. Once the fruit has cooled, pour the excess sauce into a separate bowl.

Remove the crusts from the sliced bread and cut each slice into 3 equal sized rectangles.

Dip the sliced bread into the excess sauce and allow to soak up the sauce, line each dariole with the strips slightly overlapping until the entire inside is lined.

Once the moulds are lined, fill with the softened berries, pour in a little of the excess sauce and cover with a disc of soaked bread.

Cover each mould with cling film and then place a weight on top of them; this will help the puddings to set up, place into a fridge for at least 2 to 3 hours – for best results leave overnight.

To serve:

Gently slide a small knife around the inside of the dariole to loosen; gently shake from its mould and plate as desired.

Garnish with some of the raspberry purée, a selection of mixed berries – finish with a sprig of mint and lightly dust with icing sugar. Serve the double cream in a sauce boat and allow your guests to help themselves.

The Living Room

Unit 4, Regency Wharf, 2 Broad St, Birmingham B1 2JZ
Tel: 0870 4422539
www.thelivingroom.co.uk

Malmaison

Group Operations Chef, Ray Brown (left) and Head Chef, Patrick Harness

Malmaison Birmingham opened its doors in 2002, located in the super-stylish Mailbox development. Originally Malmaison was a brasserie and bar with rooms for guests that came to dine. Ten years later, the brasseries are still a huge draw for locals and overnight guests alike and are the heart and soul of each Malmaison – always buzzy, bustling and friendly.

With traditional grills, brasserie classics and reflective of contemporary tastes, we are serious about wine, passionate about food. I was the opening head chef and now oversee all of the Malmaison hotel kitchens, continuing to offer a traditional brasserie dining experience with a modern twist and plenty of charisma!

Malmaison Birmingham offers a beautifully designed modern brasserie, with plenty of natural light and full of little pockets of privacy surrounded by walls lined with wine bottles, a private dining room for those intimate parties and a wine cellar which offers Vine Dining – where you can meet the personalities behind the labels.

Ray Brown, Group Operations Chef

Onion soup gratinée

Makes 12 portions

Ingredients

2¹/₂kg Spanish onions	300ml white wine
50g butter	100ml port
50ml olive oil	8l chicken stock
30g garlic, crushed	12 baguette slices
10g thyme	200g Gruyère, grated
4 bay leaves	Seasoning

Method

Melt butter and olive oil in a thick-bottomed pan.

Thinly slice onions and add to the pan. Cook at a medium temperature, stirring frequently to prevent burning, sauté until they reach a caramelised, dark brown colour, but are not burnt.

Add the crushed garlic, chopped thyme, bay leaves, salt and pepper; cook for a further 10 – 15 minutes.

Raise the heat to high and add the white wine, bring to the boil, then reduce by half.

Add the chicken stock and simmer for 45 minutes.

Remove bay leaves and add the port. Season to taste.

Toast the baguette croutes (slices), place on top of the soup in a lion head soup bowl. Cover with grated Gruyère and grill until melted and golden.

Serve immediately.

Malmaison

1 Wharfside St, The Mailbox, Birmingham B1 1RD
Tel: 0121 246 5000
www.malmaison.com

Roasted fillet of cod with Parma ham and vegetable broth

180g cod fillet (per portion)

For the broth:
500g Parma ham trimmings
$^1/_2$ onion
$^1/_2$ carrot
2 sticks of celery
2l chicken stock or water
(The above to be made into stock)

For the garnish:
2 carrots, diced
2 sticks of celery, diced
200g broad beans
2 leeks, diced
Plenty of freshly chopped herbs

Method

First make your stock and prepare all of your vegetables.

To prepare your cod lay two fillets top to tail and tie with string to form a barrel. Leave to rest in fridge before cutting into portions.

Now simply roast your cut portions (180g) through the oven at 175°C for 10 minutes, remembering to keep it slightly opaque in the middle.

Now for the broth; re-heat enough for however many portions you are preparing and when boiling add plenty of the diced vegetables with a good knob of butter and a good pinch of chopped herbs. Season.

Pour the broth into a large pasta bowl with the fish on top and serve.

Malmaison

1 Wharfside St, The Mailbox, Birmingham B1 1RD
Tel: 0121 246 5000
www.malmaison.com

Chocolate fondue

Ingredients

For the marshmallows:

350g sugar

1tbsps glucose

15ml water

3 leaves gelatine

2 egg whites

Chocolate sauce:

400g dark chocolate

500ml double cream

100ml milk

Fruit to serve:

150g diced pineapple

1 mango

1 punnet strawberries

1 banana

1 kiwi fruit

1 punnet of blackberries

Method

For the marshmallows:

Boil sugar, glucose and water while soaking gelatine.

Whisk egg whites to stiff peak.

Slowly pour the syrup into the egg whites then add gelatine.

Add food colouring if needed.

Spread evenly onto silicon paper and chill until needed.

When cutting up the marshmallows use $1/2$ icing sugar and $1/2$ corn flour mixed together to dredge the cut marshmallows.

For the chocolate sauce:

Bring cream and milk to boil and pour over the chopped chocolate then cover with cling film and leave to stand for 10 minutes.

Remove cling film and stir.

Reserve till needed.

Malmaison

1 Wharfside St, The Mailbox, Birmingham B1 1RD
Tel: 0121 246 5000
www.malmaison.com

The Oriental Bar Restaurant

Head Chef, Alan Chew

Set alongside the canal with stunning views, the restaurant is situated in Birmingham's prestigious Mailbox and is within easy walking distance of the ICC on Broad Street and China Town.

The bar is the perfect spot for business meetings, or to unwind after a hard afternoon at work or shopping. Accompanied with the view we have a great range of wines, beers, sake and cocktails. We also have a bar menu that provides a variety of Oriental tapas, noodles, soups and set menus for lunches.

With a focus on fine food and wine, service and style, this innovative restaurant and bar brings together dishes from Malaysia, Thailand and China.

This is the only fine dining restaurant in the city to offer authentic Malaysian cuisine. Our talented chefs are masters at creating culinary speciality delights like Beef Rendang, Nasi Gorneg, Sambal Ayam, Tom Yam soup, Thai Green Curry, Fried Seafood in XO sauce, all of which are presented on beautifully decorated plates created by our food carving specialist from Thailand.

Open from 12pm to 11pm everyday, whether for business, pleasure or to spend a lazy afternoon relaxing with a glass of wine by the canal side, The Oriental Bar Restaurant is the spot in Birmingham to – eat – drink – chill out.

George Kattapuram

Malaysian BBQ king prawns

Serves 2

100ml lemon juice

100ml fish sauce

5 tbsps of sugar

10 small chillies

10 cloves of fresh garlic

1 tsp fresh coriander

1 tsp pickled garlic

8 king prawns with shell

Method

Butterfly the king prawns (as shown, right) and grill them for 3-4 minutes.

For the dipping sauce:
Chop the fresh chillies, garlic, pickled garlic and coriander into very fine pieces. Add lemon juice, fish sauce and sugar. Mix it together.

Lay the fresh grilled king prawns on a serving plate. Pour the sauce into a dipping dish.

Perfect for parties.

The Oriental Bar Restaurant

128-130 Wharfside Street, The Mailbox, Birmingham B1 1RQ
Tel: 0121 633 9988
www.theoriental.uk.com

Hot & sour pineapple cod – Nanas Assam cod

Ingredients

450g of cod, filleted with skin off	1 tsp sugar
100g pineapple chunks	1 stick lemon grass
10 tbsps Tamarind juice (Tamarind is available from any Chinese supermarket)	4 red chillies
	4 shallots
	100ml water
1 tbsp salt	2 tbsps vegetable oil

Method

For the paste:

Place the lemon grass stick, red chillies, half the tamarind, sugar, salt and shallots into a blender; blend until it becomes a paste.

Dice the cod into pieces of 2 inch square.

Place two tablespoons of oil into a hot wok and add the paste and cook for 2 minutes. Add the water, the rest of the Tamarind juice and bring to boil. Add the cod and pineapple and simmer until the fish is cooked – approx 10 minutes – and serve. This is best accompanied with steamed rice.

The Oriental Bar Restaurant

128-130 Wharfside Street, The Mailbox, Birmingham B1 1RQ
Tel: 0121 633 9988
www.theoriental.uk.com

Malaysian spicy crab

For the sauce:

250ml water

4 tsps red chilli sauce

2 tsps tomato ketchup

2 tsps sugar

1 tsp salt

For the crab:

1 red chilli

1 spring onion

1 tsp vegetable oil

1 large prepared crab with claws

Fresh parsley and chilli (to garnish)

Method

To make the sauce:

Mix all ingredients together until they are blended well together.

Steaming the crab:

Place the crab in a steamer for about 3-4 minutes.

Chop the chilli into small fine rings; chop spring onions into fine round rings.

Add 1 teaspoon of vegetable oil into a hot wok. Add chopped chilli and spring onions, mix the sauce into the wok and stir. When the sauce starts to boil remove from the heat.

Remove the crab from the steamer, drain any excess water, then place the crab on serving dish. Dress the crab with the sauce and garnish with fresh parsley and chilli.

The Oriental Bar Restaurant

128-130 Wharfside Street, The Mailbox, Birmingham B1 1RQ
Tel: 0121 633 9988
www.theoriental.uk.com

Red Peppers

Colette Whelan,
Operations Director

Red Peppers is situated in The Mailbox, opposite its sister restaurant Bar Estilo.

Its bright and colourful interior makes a perfect setting for relaxed and casual dining.

The menu is an eclectic array of different styles and flavours, where old favourites sit comfortably next to new dishes from around the world. The varied menu and relaxed atmosphere make Red Peppers the perfect choice for any occasion. The wine list offers a selection of old and new world wines to complement all the flavours of the menu and there's a bar for a pre-dinner cocktail should you be in the mood.

Red Peppers opens from noon everyday and serves throughout the afternoon. It also has a sunny terrace for alfresco dining – weather permitting of course!

Colette Whelan
Operations Director

Goat's cheese and tarragon tarts

Serves 6

For the filling:

250g goat's cheese

125g Mascarpone

15g fresh tarragon (finely chopped)

50g semi-dried tomatoes (chopped)

$\frac{1}{2}$ tsp salt

$\frac{1}{2}$ tsp black pepper

2 egg yolks

For the shortcrust pastry:

200g plain flour

Pinch of salt

60g butter

40g solid vegetable fat

3-4 tbsps ice cold water

Method

To make the pastry:

Sieve the flour and salt. Cut up the butter and fat and add to the flour. Rub the fat into the flour with fingertips until it resembles breadcrumbs.

Add about half the water to start and mix quickly with a table knife. The pastry should start to come together, add more water a few drops at a time if required, finally bring the dough together using your fingertips and mould into a ball.

Cover and leave in the refrigerator to rest for half an hour. Cut pastry into six even pieces and roll out into circles on a floured surface to fit tartlet tins.

Grease the tartlet tins and carefully line with the pastry. Bake blind in a preheated oven at 200°C for approx 8-10 minutes. Remove and allow to cool.

To make the tart:

Break up the goat's cheese into a mixing bowl and add all other ingredients. Mix well to combine all ingredients together. Divide the mixture between the tartlets. (At this stage you can refrigerate until needed or bake for service.)

Return the tartlets to the oven and bake for 10-12 minutes until golden brown on top.

To serve:

Garnish with a few dressed salad leaves and some caramelised onions.

Red Peppers

117 Wharfside Street, The Mailbox, Birmingham B1 1RF
Tel: 0121 643 4202

Fishcakes with mint and pea salad, lemon and herb mayonnaise

Ingredients

Fishcakes:

200g salmon

200g cod

200g smoked haddock

(All fish should be skinned and filleted)

500g potatoes

1 onion (finely chopped)

75g butter

1 tbsp dill (finely chopped)

2 tbsps flat leaf parsley (finely chopped)

2 lemons (zest only)

1 tsp salt

1 tsp pepper

For the breadcrumb coating:

40g flour

1 lemon (zest only)

1 tbsp parsley (finely chopped)

150g white breadcrumbs

2 eggs

Oil for frying

Lemon and herb mayonnaise:

250ml mayonnaise

1 lemon (juice only)

10g chives (finely chopped)

10g dill (finely chopped)

Mint and pea salad:

50g mixed baby salad leaves

150g sugar snap peas

150g fresh podded peas

25g fresh mint leaves

Pinch salt

Pinch caster sugar

Pinch pepper

$^1/_2$ lemon (juice only)

1 tbsp olive oil

Method

To make the fishcakes:

Cook the potatoes, drain and mash with 50g butter. Season with salt and pepper. Cover the fish with water, bring to the boil and remove from the heat immediately and drain off the water.

Sauté the onion in 25g butter until cooked but not browned. Mix together the potato, herbs, lemon zest and onion, then flake in the fish. Check the seasoning and mould into eight cakes.

Combine the breadcrumbs with the parsley and lemon zest. Beat the eggs. Dip each fishcake firstly in flour, then the egg and then the breadcrumbs.

Heat the oil in a frying pan and cook the fishcakes over a medium heat for a few minutes each side until golden. Transfer to a baking tray and cook in preheated oven at 200°C for about 10 minutes.

Mint and pea salad:

Cook the sugar snap peas in salted boiling water for 2-3 minutes only. Cook the garden peas in boiling salted water for approx 10 - 15 minutes until tender.

Once cooked drain and cool the peas immediately under cold water. Place in a mixing bowl and add sugar, salt, pepper, lemon juice and oil.

Mix until the salt and sugar dissolve. Tear in the mint leaves and toss gently with the baby leaves. Serve immediately.

Lemon and herb mayonnaise:

Mix all ingredients together. Refrigerate until needed.

To serve:

Once the fishcakes are cooked, place on serving plates with the mint salad. Serve the mayonnaise separately.

Red Peppers

117 Wharfside Street, The Mailbox, Birmingham B1 1RF

Tel: 0121 643 4202

Chocolate parfait with fresh raspberries and cream

Serves 6-8

200g dark bitter chocolate

2 egg yolks

2 whole eggs

50g caster sugar

1 tsp vanilla essence

2 tbsp cognac

125ml whipping cream

500ml double cream

Punnet of raspberries

Break the chocolate into small pieces. Melt in a mixing bowl over a pan of simmering water. Once melted leave to cool for a couple of minutes. Beat the whole eggs and the yolks with the sugar until pale and thick.

In a separate bowl whisk the whipping cream until thick.

Add the melted chocolate to the beaten egg and sugar and whisk until completely combined. Whisk in the cognac and vanilla essence. Gently fold the cream into the chocolate mixture.

Line a 500g loaf tin with cling film and pour in the mixture. Place in the freezer overnight.

To serve

Remove from the freezer and place in the refrigerator approx 20 minutes before service to soften slightly.

Turn out the parfait onto a plate and remove cling film. Slice and place on serving plates.

Pour over the double cream and place 6-8 raspberries on each plate.

Red Peppers

**117 Wharfside Street, The Mailbox, Birmingham B1 1RF
Tel: 0121 643 4202**

Simpsons

Executive Chef, Luke Tipping

Since opening in 2004, Simpsons has swiftly become one of the most acclaimed restaurants in Birmingham.

Located in fashionable Edgbaston, this fine, early Victorian villa is beautifully presented, with tall windows and a delightfully secluded garden with terrace, suitable for sumptuous alfresco dining. With four luxuriously individual en-suite bedrooms, a cookery school and private dining room, Simpsons offers more than just the allure of its dining rooms.

Restaurateur Andreas Antona built his reputation at the original Simpsons in Kenilworth, where he won a coveted Michelin star which he now holds at the flagship Edgbaston restaurant. Simpsons has once again been recognised, by being awarded the Best Restaurant in Birmingham at the Taste of Birmingham Awards, where Andreas was also presented with an award for outstanding contribution to the restaurant industry.

Alongside Andreas, Executive Chef Luke Tipping and Head Chef Adam Bennett present light, modern dishes made from beautifully fresh ingredients based on classical French cuisine.

Simpsons is open for both lunch and dinner Monday to Saturday and lunch only on Sundays. We look forward to welcoming you to Simpsons!

Salcombe crab cocktail

For the Granny Smith jelly:

300ml freshly pressed Granny Smith apple juice

Juice of ½ lemon

30g sugar

2 leaves gelatine soaked in cold water for 10 minutes

For the crab mixture:

4 tbsps of picked white crab meat (ours is from Salcombe)

2 tbsps mayonnaise

1 tsp lemon juice

For the apple Purée:

6 Cox's apples-peeled, cored and diced

½ tbsp sugar

1 tsp lemon juice

Apple foam:

250g Cox's apple purée (see above)

100ml double cream

1 leaf of gelatine soaked in cold water for 10 minutes

Method

For the Granny Smith jelly:

Add the lemon juice to the apple juice to prevent discolouration. Warm 75ml of the juice with the sugar to dissolve, then stir in the gelatine. Stir the gelatine mixture into the rest of the juice and pass it through a fine sieve. Pour a little jelly into each of the four glasses to give a layer of about 1½ cm in depth. Chill for about an hour or until set.

NB The glasses should be of about 135ml capacity.

For the crab mixture:

Mix all the ingredients together, the consistency should be soft not runny. Spoon a little crab mixture into the glasses to cover the jelly. Fill within 1cm of the rim of the glass. Reserve in the fridge.

For the apple purée:

Cook all of the ingredients gently in a pan with a tight fitting lid until soft. Purée in a liquidiser until smooth. Measure 250g and set aside for the foam; spread a little of the remaining purée on top of the crab in each glass.

Apple foam:

Bring the cream to the boil and remove from the heat. Immediately add the drained gelatine, stir to dissolve. Combine the cream mixture with the apple puree then cool the mixture. When the mixture is cool, whip to a light fluffy consistency.

To serve:

Remove the glasses from the fridge 10 minutes before serving to raise the temperature slightly; too cold and the flavours will be somewhat dulled. Just before serving top each with the apple foam. At Simpsons we also add a few baby salad leaves and a crisp apple wafer, but it will be delicious even without these.

Simpsons

20 Highfield Road, Edgbaston, Birmingham B15 3DX
Tel: 0121 454 3434
www.simpsonsrestaurant.co.uk

Sea bream with potato scales, creamed leeks, red wine sauce

Ingredients

For the fish:

4 x 200g skinless bream fillets
2 tbsps potato flour
16 Ratte potatoes (or another variety of waxy potato)
200ml clarified butter

The sauce:

300ml red wine
200ml veal stock
300ml fish stock
50g chopped shallots
60g sliced button mushroom
50ml double cream
200g diced butter

The creamed leeks:

3 leeks, trimmed
1 tbsp olive oil
15g butter
150ml double cream
$\frac{1}{2}$ tsp curry powder

Method

Coat the bream fillets with the potato flour and place on a tray. Peel and slice the potatoes with a Japonaise mandolin lengthways to a thickness of about 1mm (if you do not have a mandolin, simply slice thinly). From the slices cut enough tiny discs with a pastry cutter or apple corer, 10mm is ideal to cover the bream fillets in overlapping rows. When all four portions have been covered with the potato scales, brush each with clarified butter to seal the potatoes and keep them in place. Place the fish in the fridge to set the butter hard until it is time to cook.

To make the sauce:

Combine all the ingredients except the cream and butter. Reduce over high heat until slightly syrupy; add butter and cream bring to the boil. Strain it through a sieve into a clean pan, season and taste.

For the leeks:

Thinly slice the leeks and wash well. Heat the olive oil and butter in a frying pan, add the leeks and season with salt and curry powder. Cook without colour (ie gently without browning) for 5 minutes until tender, stir in cream and heat through.

Heat a non-stick pan large enough to take two bream fillets. Gently place the bream in the pan potato side down. Cook over a moderate heat to give a really crisp finish to the potato scales. When the potatoes are crispy, season the fish and carefully turn the fish over. Turn off the heat and leave to cook in its residual heat, keep warm. Repeat for last two bream fillets.

To serve:

Place an 8cm pastry cutter on each of the 4 warmed plates, spoon the leek mixture into the 4 rings. Place fish to one side, spoon sauce around, season the potato scales and serve.

Simpsons

20 Highfield Road, Edgbaston, Birmingham B15 3DX
Tel: 0121 454 3434
www.simpsonsrestaurant.co.uk

Amaretti macaroon, poached cherries, Valrhona Ivoire chocolate sorbet, Morello cherry granite

This recipe requires an ice cream maker and some silicon paper

Ingredients

For the macaroons:

60g ground almonds	
110g icing sugar	
15g caster sugar	
55g egg whites	
2 tbsp crushed amaretti biscuits	

For the white chocolate sorbet:
(This amount will serve more than 4 people but can be kept in the freezer for next time)

270ml warm water	
35g milk powder	
45g glucose liquid	
10g sugar	
135g Valrhona Ivoire white chocolate	

For the poached cherries:

Approximately 20 cherries stoned (more if they are small)

300ml red wine	
60g caster sugar	
1 inch stick of cinnamon	
1 strip of orange zest	

For the Morello cherry granite:

100g Morello cherries (stoned)	
125ml cherry poaching liquor (see above)	

Method

For the macaroons:

Sift the almonds with the icing sugar and reserve. Whisk the egg whites with the caster sugar until firm. Fold the two mixtures together, place the mix in a piping bag with ½ inch plain nozzle. Pipe onto silicon paper in discs of about 3 inches in diameter, sprinkle each one with amaretti biscuits. Bake at 140°C for 12-15 minutes, cool and reserve.

For the white chocolate sorbet:

Mix all ingredients together, heat gently to 85°C stirring all the time. Remove from the heat and pass through a fine sieve and chill. Churn in an ice cream machine and reserve in the freezer.

For the poached cherries:

Bring the wine, sugar, cinnamon and orange zest to the boil and simmer for 5 minutes to dissolve. Add the cherries to the simmering syrup, return to the boil then remove from the heat. Leave to cool in the syrup. Once cool, drain the cherries in a small sieve and reserve the liquor for the granite.

For the Morello cherry granite:

Mix the cherries and liquor, purée in a liquidizer until smooth then pass through a fine sieve. Pour into a freezer-proof container and place in the freezer. Stir every 25 minutes until you have a nice granular texture. Reserve in the freezer.

To serve:

Choose four perfect macaroons and reserve. Break two others into small pieces. Place a quarter of the macaroon pieces in the centre of four plates with a scoop of white chocolate sorbet on top. Rest a macaroon behind the ice cream and five cherries around the side with a spoonful of granite alongside. Serve immediately.

Simpsons

20 Highfield Road, Edgbaston, Birmingham B15 3DX
Tel: 0121 454 3434
www.simpsonsrestaurant.co.uk

Thai Edge

Head Chef, Mit Jeensanthai

Thai Edge provides the very best in award-winning Thai cuisine in a specially designed, contemporary setting providing a most exciting and memorable dining experience. Gone are the heavily themed, crimson shades and cluttered environments that are typical of Oriental eateries. They are replaced by an approach that gives great emphasis to clean crisp lines, balance and intelligent use of space.

Thai cuisine is popular for its subtle blending of flavours, utilising herbs and roots such as lemon grass, basil, coriander, galangal, krachai, ginger, garlic and chillies.

Our menu showcases four different traditional styles of Thai cooking, each prepared, cooked and presented in perfect harmony with the surroundings.

Northern cuisine is rich and mild, making good use of coconut milk, while North Eastern cuisine is spicier, influenced by Laos and Cambodia.

Chinese-inspired Central cuisine is good for people with a milder palate, and concentrates on the use of coconut, lemon and basil leaves, while Southern cuisine – the spiciest food of all – is influenced by Malaysia and India. No matter which of the extensive choice of 145 dishes you pick from our menu we guarantee a complete Thai culinary experience.

Head chef Mit Jeensanthai (Taiman) brings with him the recipes and techniques, perfected through years of experience, that give Thai Edge its authentic taste of Thailand.

Tom Yum prawns

Serves 2

Ingredients

1kg fresh prawns

2 stalks lemon grass, bruised (this isn't eaten, but is an essential flavouring)

2 kaffir lime leaves (use lime zest if you can't get it)

2 coriander (cilantro) plants, chopped

10-15 prik ki nu (birdseye chillies), thinly sliced

10 button mushroons, cut into convenient spoonable pieces

2-5 dried red chillies

Juice of 3 or 4 limes

2-3 tbsps sliced bamboo shoots or coconut shoots

2-3 tbsps fish sauce

1-2 tbsps chillies in oil

Method

The fresh chillies should be bruised in a mortar and pestle. The dried chillies should be heated first, then crumbled into the fresh chillies. Beat the lemon grass with the grinder of the mortar and pestle.

Heat about 3 cups of water in a saucepan to boiling point, add all the ingredients, and stir constantly until cooked (it doesn't take long for mushrooms, but longer for chicken or shrimp, and longest if you use beef instead of prawns).

Variation: Use three cups of thin coconut milk instead of water, the result is called Tom Kha, rather than Tom Yum.

Thai Edge

7 Oozells Square, Brindleyplace, Birmingham B1 2HL
Tel: 0121 643 3993
www.thaiedge.co.uk

Lamb Penang

1kg lamb, cut into bite sized pieces

300ml coconut milk

1 tbsp chopped garlic

2-3 tbsps Penang curry paste

2 tbsps fish sauce

Sugar to taste

3 kaffir lime leaves, shredded

10-15 Thai basil leaves, finely shredded

Method

Place a wok over medium high heat, and warm the coconut milk (do not allow to boil). Add the curry paste, and stir it until the oil begins to separate out and form a thin film. To bring out the maximum flavour, add the remaining ingredients except the lime leaves and basil leaves, and simmer until the sauce is absorbed and thickened. Add the lime leaves and basil leaves and stir fry briefly before serving.

Garnish with julienned red chilli, with Thai jasmine rice, and the usual Thai table condiments.

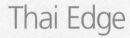

Thai Edge

7 Oozells Square, Brindleyplace, Birmingham B1 2HL
Tel: 0121 643 3993
www.thaiedge.co.uk

Thai sea bass

Serves 2

1.5kg sea bass

For the Thai sauce:

Zest and juice of 3 limes

3 tbsps fresh ginger, grated

1/2 cup soy sauce

3 tbsps vegetable oil

4 cloves garlic, minced

1/2 tsp red pepper flakes

Method

Prepare the Thai sauce recipe by combining all the sauce ingredients in a medium bowl.

Coat the fish pieces well with the sauce and grill over medium heat for about 10 minutes each side, or until the fish is opaque and flakes easily with a fork. Baste often.

Thai Edge

7 Oozells Square, Brindleyplace, Birmingham B1 2HL
Tel: 0121 643 3993
www.thaiedge.co.uk

Turner's Grill

Turner's
GRILL

Executive Chef, John Stephens

It is amazing how many people 'in the know' say that the best food is freshly prepared, simple and cooked with care and attention. At Turner's Grill, opened in partnership with the Copthorne Hotel Birmingham, not only do we believe that, it's what we do.

The restaurant has been simply yet elegantly converted to give a grill room feel.

Mirrors, pictures and a wooden floor add to the homely feel of the place. The menu is simple and to my mind decently priced. Great quality produce converted to tasty dishes to tax no-one after a hard day's work, whether you are away from home or living locally.

The welcome and friendliness of the team within the grill, led by Phil Clayton, and the skill and dedication of the kitchen with John Stephens in control, combine to give a great experience to everyone who joins us.

So come on, you know it makes sense, we would love to see you soon – enjoy!

Brian Turner CBE

Leek salad with soft boiled egg

Serves 2

Ingredients

1kg tender young leeks	30ml red wine vinegar	**For the Cheshire cheese dressing:**
4 medium organic fresh eggs	1 finely chopped shallot	
Maldon Salt (available in most supermarkets	5g finely chopped olive	50g finely grated Cheshire cheese
	5g finely chopped parsley	25ml virgin olive oil
	10g Dijon mustard	10ml white wine vinegar
For the vinaigrette:	Pepper	25ml single cream
75ml grapeseed oil	Salt	Garlic clove, crushed to a paste
30ml sherry vinegar		10g finely chopped tarragon

Method

Wash and trim the leeks. Tie into bundles, bring a large pan of salted water to the boil. Cook the leeks for just under 10 minutes until tender but not too soft.

Remove and refresh for 15 seconds only, drain and lay on a towel to dry.

For the vinaigrette:
To make the vinaigrette, whisk all the ingredients together, pour over the leeks whilst they are still tepid. Allow to cool naturally.

For the cheese dressing:
Put the cheese in a food processor, gradually add the oil and then the vinegar, beating all the time. Then add the cream, garlic and tarragon to produce a smooth, creamy dressing.

For the egg:
On the bottom of the egg, pierce with a sharp knife point. Place the eggs gently into a pan of boiling water for 3-4 minutes, remove from the water and gently refresh, then peel.

To reheat, place in boiling water for 30 seconds until warm but soft.

Alternatively, dip the peeled egg in flour, milk and breadcrumbs and deep fry for 30 seconds (see picture).

To serve:
Place the leeks attractively on a plate (8 per portion), drizzle with the cheese dressing. Place the soft egg in the centre, top with a little Maldon salt and serve. You can add extra garnish (pictured) of an onion ring (sliced, soaked in milk, drain and toss in flour with paprika and seasoning, deep fry at 180°C) and some tomato – skinned, seeded, quartered and diced.

Turner's Grill

Copthorne Hotel Birmingham
Paradise Circus, Birmingham B3 3HJ
0121 200 2727

Belly of pork with black vinegar and char-grilled vegetables

Ingredients

For the pork:

1kg thick pork belly, skinned and boned

1 star anise, crushed

10 crushed juniper berries

15 crushed black peppercorns

2.5cm fresh ginger

30ml olive oil

2 onions, cut in halves

4 carrots, cut lengthways

2 leeks, cut into 2.5cm pieces

2 garlic cloves

4 sprigs of rosemary

4 sprigs of thyme

2 bay leaves

1 litre chicken stock

For the black vinegar:

100ml balsamic vinegar

50ml white wine vinegar

30g caster sugar

1 shallot, peeled and finely chopped

20ml honey

For the grilled vegetables:

1 large aubergine, cut into 12 slices

3 red peppers, seeded and cut into quarters

24 large button mushrooms, stems removed

3 courgettes, cut thick diagonally

30ml olive oil

1 lime, juiced

5g fresh coriander, finely chopped

Salt, pepper

For the marinade:

45ml soy sauce

25ml olive oil

2 garlic cloves, crushed

10g paprika

10g ground cumin

Splash of Tabasco sauce

Method

For the pork:

Rub the pork with the crushed seasoning (star anise, peppercorns, juniper berries and ginger), add a little sea salt, roll and tie neatly.

Heat the oil and sear the pork, set aside.

Fry all the trimmings from the pork (the fat and bones) in hot oil until brown and crispy, remove from the pan and add the vegetables (carrots, onions, leeks); cook for 1 minute.

Place the pork on top.

Add the herbs and pour enough stock to cover, bring to the boil and remove scum.

Cover the meat and cook in the oven, 170°C for 3-4 hours. Once the meat is tender, remove from the pan, remove the string and roll tightly in cling film – chill until it has set.

Pass the sauce and boil it until it forms a syrup.

To serve, cut pork into thick medallions, rub with a little oil and sear on the char grill; heat a little of the sauce, place the pork in it and place into the oven until heated through.

Serve on top of the char-grilled vegetables.

For the vinegar:

Place all the ingredients in a non-reactive pan.

Reduce to a syrup, adjust the flavour and consistency as required. Use this as plate dressing.

For the vegetables:

Make the marinade and mix it with 45ml water, brush the aubergine with some of the marinade.

Mix the marinade with the remaining vegetables in a large bowl, leave in a cool place for at least an hour.

Grill the vegetables for 3-4 minutes until they pick up colour. Combine the olive oil, lime juice, coriander and salt and pepper and trickle over the cooked vegetables. Serve with the pork.

Turner's Grill

Copthorne Hotel Birmingham
Paradise Circus, Birmingham B3 3HJ
0121 200 2727

Hot treacle tart with vanilla ice cream

This recipe requires an ice cream maker

For the filling:

600ml whipping cream

600ml golden syrup

Zest and juice of 2 lemons

4 apples – peeled, cored, finely diced

10 whole eggs

Orange flower water to taste

200g crushed cornflakes

For the ice cream:

300ml double cream

300ml milk

1 vanilla pod

6 egg yolks

175g caster sugar

For the pastry case:

1kg flour

400g icing sugar

5g salt

400g butter

250g eggs

For the tart filling:

Place the cream, syrup, lemon zest and juice, apples and orange flower water into a pan, bring to the boil, simmer for 5 minutes and then chill right down.

Add the eggs, making sure it is all well mixed.

Line a 25cm tart case with your rolled out pastry (see below), 4mm thick, and then fill with the finely crushed cornflakes and then top up with the filling mixture.

Bake at 140°C for 20-30 minutes or until lightly set.

For the pastry:

Mix the flour, butter, icing sugar and salt together. Add the eggs – don't overwork (it can be done in a food processor) and rest for 20 minutes.

For the ice cream:

Mix together the cream and milk, add the split vanilla pod, bring to the boil. Cream the yolks and the sugar, add the cream mix.

Return to the pan and cook out slowly. Do not curdle.

Once thickened, pass through a fine sieve and cool.

Once cool, churn until frozen.

Turner's Grill

Copthorne Hotel Birmingham
Paradise Circus, Birmingham B3 3HJ
0121 200 2727

House Of Fraser
Foodhall

House of Fraser Food Hall
– a tasty destination

House of Fraser Birmingham's Food Hall is a celebration of food where customers can select from light bites, deli delights, gorgeous gifts and enjoy all the pleasures of eating in or selecting inspiring ingredients for cooking at home.

Whether you're a businessman-on-the-go needing a quick lunchtime fix, a savvy shopper seeking a re-energising pit-stop or a social soul wanting to relax with friends over a meal and a glass of Chablis, our state-of-the-art Food Hall is the perfect location for you. There are food sensations from around the world to choose from Europe to India and South East Asia. There are quick bites and delicious meals from tantalising tapas to classic curry, perfect pies to nourishing noodles, all freshly prepared before you.

Celebrate in style with a glass of Champagne

Whether celebrating with friends, setting the scene for a night of romance, or simply treating yourself with a wonderfully indulgent tipple; there's nothing more satisfying than a glass of Champagne. Match the moment with a Champagne to suit the occasion from House of Fraser.

For a flavoursome all-rounder try Champagne Billecart-Salmon Non Vintage. Clean, fresh, with a delicately well-balanced array of flavours, this Champagne is perfect for any occasion. Entertaining? Complement your cooking skills with Champagne Bollinger Special Cuvée Non Vintage. One of the few Champagnes that has its first fermentation conducted in an oak barrel, this process adds power and substance to a classic Champagne. Excellent as an aperitif or as an accompaniment to fish and white meat.

Wind down with a glass of wine…

Choose from our list of thrilling wines from around the world. Whether you're looking for a crisp white, fruity rosé or smooth red, House of Fraser has a great selection of quality wines at prices that are easy on the purse.

Chardonnay, Rioja or Sauvignon Blanc, relax with a post-work fruity white wine. Rayen Chardonnay from Chile has a delicate aroma of

tropical fruit and bananas. Looking for a wine with a deep character? Vergelegen Sauvignon Blanc from South Africa has an intensity that comes from its relatively high fermentation temperature. House of Fraser Senior Wine Buyer James Taylor advises: "This wine is the perfect accompaniment to seafood, a nose of gooseberries, fig and elderflower leads to a balanced wine with a long finish worth savouring."

Rosé lovers will appreciate R.H Phillips White Zindanfel from California. The grapes for this wine are harvested in the dark of night, helping to retain the acidity and freshness of the fruit. Enjoy the multitude of sweet flavours – strawberry, cranberry and watermelon, which make this wine an ideal aperitif. If you're looking for a great summer wine, try homegrown English Chapel Down Rosé, an elaborate mix of Pinot Noir, Dornfelder, Rondo, Madaline Angevine, Seyval Blanc

and Schönberger. With a fruity bouquet of strawberries this is great picnic wine, and at a great price too.

Love to wax lyrical with a great glass of red? Try Lizard Flat Shiraz, all the way from South Australia. Gold Medal Award winning, its rich full flavour of blackberries, spice and plums, coupled with such a rare depth and intensity, belies its great value price. Organic of mind? To be classed as an organic wine, not only do the grapes have to be grown organically – but the whole production has to be kept under strict sterile conditions. De Martino Organic Cabernet Sauvignon originates from Chile and is a well balanced, full bodied wine with integrated oak. Taste with red meat, followed by a variety of cheeses (organic of course) for best effect!

James Taylor,
Senior Wine Buyer

Deli delights

Spoil yourself with some take-home treats and try some of House of Fraser's enticing delicacies – select from cold meats, antipasti, fine cheeses and a delicious

range of breads and flavoursome accompaniments. Planning an Italian extravaganza? Select from succulent meats, like Salsiccia al Finocchio sausage, Milano Salami and Pancetta Affumicata, or spice it up with Artisan Chorizo sausage meat, accompanied with some warm, freshly baked foccacia, large olives stuffed with garlic, almonds or anchovies and a bottle or two of Zinfandel or Pinot Grigio. From the boardroom to the desk, sandwich platters can be freshly made for the entire team or just one or two for you from rocket and pastrami, Mexican roast vegetables or smoked salmon and dill crème fraiche!

Cheese

From Gloucestershire to the Auvergne, from sheep's to goat's, House of Fraser has a wonderful selection of specialist cheeses and savoury crackers. Anglophiles can choose from the soft, fresh lemony Cerney Ash Pyramid goat's cheese made in Gloucestershire, deep-flavoured Greens Cheddar matured for 14 months in Somerset, to nutty flavoured Berkswell hard sheep's cheese from Warwickshire perfect on our celery crackers.

For a taste of the Continent, choose Picos di Europa, a Spanish cheese from La Mancha wrapped in Sycamore leaves with an intense, long-lasting blue flavour, Bleu

d'Auvergne, a classic French cheese with a deep and satisfying sweet flavour, or pick up a Camembert in a wooden box to bake at home for a melting taste treat – a scrumptious dip for potatoes or bread. Visit our cheese counter to try before you buy, sample, select and savour.

Luxury chocolates and confectionery

Chocolate lovers, gift givers and sweet seekers will revel in our selection.

Customers can make up a box of their own choice from a fabulous selection of great value, rich, loose Belgian chocolates or choose our own brand of pre-packed, gift wrapped boxes of superb Belgian chocolates at very competitive prices.

Sweets not found on the high street include Hershey's bars, 3 Musketeers bars, Baby Ruth bars, Tootsie Rolls and Charms.

Jelly Belly, the infamous jelly bean brand, provides the perfect sugar fix with 50 fabulous flavours including toasted marshmallow, juicy pear, strawberry cheesecake and pina colada.

Our bakery offers a wide selection of tempting fresh cakes including cream slices, cheesecake, gateaux and delicious tarts, assorted freshly baked breads and patisserie items such as croissants, pains au chocolat and Danish pastries.

House Of Fraser
Foodhall

Corporation Street, Birmingham B2 5JS
Tel: 0870 160 7225
www.houseoffraser.co.uk

Store cupboard (essentials to have in stock)

Basics
Rice: Basmati, arborio, brown
Mustard: Dijon, wholegrain, mustard powder
Oils: Olive, canola, vegetable, sesame, walnut
Vinegars: Red, white wine, balsamic, chinese rice
Flour: Plain, self raising
Dried chillies
Bay leaves
Root ginger
Cous cous
Salt: Sea, cooking, table

Sugar: Brown, white
Tinned tomatoes
Pulses: Borlotti, cannelloni, butter beans, chickpeas
Lentils: Brown, red
Nuts: Cashew, pistachio, walnut
Almonds: Blanched, whole, flaked, slivered
Coconut milk
Cooking chocolate and cocoa powder – 70%
Sauces: Soya, fish, oyster
Anchovies

Fresh herbs
Basil
Coriander
Rosemary
Thyme
Sage
Bay
Mint
Dill
Chervil

Spices
Curry leaves
Turmeric powder

Cinnamon powder
Clove powder
Nutmeg powder
Chilli powder
Coriander powder
Cumin seeds
Coriander seeds
Cardamom pods
Fennel seeds
Mustard seeds
Caraway seeds
Peppercorns
Garam masala
Star anise

Equipment

Recommended
Baking parchment For non-stick effect.
Cake spatula For easing out cakes from tins.
Casserole dish Preferably cast iron, 5 pint = family size.
Chinois Metal conical sieve with fine mesh.
Colander Metal, with handles.
Dariole Small cylindrical mould.
Digital scales Considered to be the most accurate.
Draining spoon Metal, longhandled.
Food processor Good quality multi-purpose, with blender.
Frying pan Eight inch and ten inch.
Grater Four-sided, easy to clean.
Ice cream maker Available with either manual or mechanized churns; can also produce frozen yoghurt, ice milk and frozen beverages.
Kitchen timer With alarm mechanism.
Knife set Good quality cook's knives, serrated, bread, paring, carving, palette, cleaver.

Large mixing bowl Plus smaller glass bowls.
Mandolin Instrument, not musical, for finely slicing.
Measuring jugs Two varying sizes.
Pastry brush For basting.
Pastry cutters Various shapes and sizes, preferably metal.
Pestle and mortar Stone, not porcelain.
Rolling pin Wooden.
Saucepans Aluminium, stainless steel, copper-based, non-stick.
Sieves Rounded/conical.
Steamer Either freestanding or saucepan top.
Sugar thermometer Essential in confectionery and some dessert making, but also useful for fat temperature.
Tins Metal baking sheet, roasting tin, flan ring, mould, cake tins, patty tins, spring form tin, loaf tin.
Whisk Balloon/electric.
Wooden spoons Different sizes, plus wooden spatula.

Cooking terms and methods

Bain-Marie A cooking method where the dish is cooked immersed in a half-filled tin or pan of boiling water.

Bake blind Pie or tart crust that you partially or completely bake before it is filled; to prebake a crust, you roll it out and put it in the pan. To keep the bottom from puffing and the sides from falling, line the crust with parchment paper or a large coffee filter, and fill it with beans or rice.

Baste To coat during cooking.

Bind To blend dry and liquid ingredients.

Blanch To briefly cook in boiling water.

Blister To heat the surface of an ingredient. For example: peppers, until the skin blisters.

Blitz To rapidly blend or heat ingredients.

Brown To cook until surface starts to brown.

Butterfly To slit a piece of food in half horizontally, cutting it almost through, so that when opened it resembles butterfly wings.

Caramelise To heat sugar or sugar syrup until it browns to a caramel colour.

Clarify Remove impurities from butter or stock by heating the liquid, then straining or skimming it.

Compote A thick purée of fruit.

Concasse Coarsely chopped ingredients.

Confit Meat cooked in own fat and then preserved encased in fat to prevent contact with air.

Consommé A light clear soup/sauce.

Coulis A light fruit sauce.

Croquant Biscuit, from French for crunchy or crisp.

Croustillant A dish either presented on, or enclosed in, a shell of pastry.

Debearded A term applying to preparation of shellfish, where little hairs have been removed.

Deglaze To heat a liquid, usually stock or wine, with pan juices as basis for gravy.

Deskirted Another shellfish term referring to trimming and cleaning of scallops.

Demiglace Rich, concentrated brown stock, can be bought ready-made.

Dice Finely chop.

Dredge To sprinkle lightly and evenly with sugar or flour.

Flambé To flame a mixture containing alcohol.

Flash-fry To quickly fry.

Fold To gently combine ingredients with a metal spoon or knife.

Glaze To coat food with egg, milk or syrup before or after cooking.

Infuse To immerse strong flavoured ingredients in hot liquid, which is then left to stand for a while eg vanilla pods in milk.

Jus A clear stock or pure fruit juice.

Knead A technique applied in perfecting dough, done by hand on a floured board.

Macerate To steep in alcohol or syrup, in order to flavour or soften.

Marinade A mixture in which meat, fish or other ingredients are soaked before cooking.

Napping To coat an item with sauce.

Noisette Small piece of meat, usually the eye of a chop.

Parboil To partly boil, from five to 15 minutes.

Poach To cook food at just below boiling point for a protracted time.

Prove The second stage in bread making, where dough is allowed to rise after shaping.

Quenelle To roll or shape into a ball.

Reduce To cook liquids down so that some of the water evaporates.

Refresh Plunging just boiled or blanched vegetables into cold water, to preserve fresh colour.

Rillette A coarse paté.

Roux The butter and flour base to sauces – flour is added to melted butter and cooked into a paste for a minute before adding liquid.

Reduce To boil rapidly to reduce liquid content and concentrate flavour.

Sauté To lightly fry.

Sear To rapidly pan-cook meat at a high temperature.

Strain To pass liquid through a sieve to free it of lumps.

Sweat To seal in a covered pan.

Terrine A layered and set loaf-shaped starter, often incorporating meat.

Turn To shape with a knife or peeler, whilst rotating, into a regular, round shape.

Whipping To beat quickly with a spoon or whisk to incorporate air.

Glossary

Allspice berry From the West Indian allspice tree. When ground, it has the aroma and taste of a combination of cinnamon, cloves, nutmeg and pepper.

Brioche A light but rich French bread/cake made with yeast dough, eggs, milk and butter.

Cardamom The seeds are contained in small pods, which you crush to remove the seeds. Strong aroma and a warm, spicy-sweet flavour.

Cane syrup Golden syrup.

Capers Pickled flower buds of a shrub native to the Mediterranean and parts of Asia. Usually bought in jars.

Chervil An aromatic herb, like tarragon, with lacy leaves.

Chilli oil Bought ready-bottled from supermarkets.

Chinese wine Available from Chinese supermarkets. Use dry sherry as substitute.

Chorizo A Spanish sausage, spicy in flavour and made of ground pork.

Celeriac Root vegetable cooked like potato, with distinctive celery taste.

Cinnamon sticks Cinnamon bark in stick form, available from good supermarkets.

Cous cous A fine cereal made from semolina.

Fish sauce Condiment used in Southeast Asian cooking to add saltiness.

Five spice powder Chinese spice containing cinnamon, cloves, fennel, star anise and Sichuan peppers.

Grapeseed oil Vegetable oil pressed from the seeds of grapes.

Kirsch A liqueur distilled from crushed cherries and their stones.

Lemon grass Stalk used in Chinese and Thai cookery. Discard outer husk and crush inner stem for lemon flavour.

Mache A green salad leaf native to Europe with dark green leaves and tangy flavour. Also called field salad, field lettuce and lamb's lettuce.

Maris Piper Versatile, good quality potato.

Mange tout Whole pea pods, eaten young and blanched.

Marsala Fortified wine produced in Marsala, Sicily.

Mascarpone Italian soft cheese, often used in desserts.

Pak choy Chinese cabbage with a mild mustard taste.

Polenta Cornmeal dish made with either coarsely, medium or finely ground dried yellow or white maize.

Port wine sauce A traditional, rich sauce, can be bought ready-prepared.

Root ginger Thick root of a tropical plant, can be frozen.

Saffron Vibrant natural colourant, extracted from crocuses.

Salmon keta A small salmon, native to the Pacific Coast of America.

Saltpeter Potassium nitrate, used in preservation of meat. Available from chemists or online.

Savoyarde/Savoiardi biscuits Traditional dessert biscuits, readily available.

Scallops Shellfish available in a range of sizes, with delicate taste.

Soy sauce Made from fermented soy beans. Use dark for extra colour, light for flavour and salty taste.

Star anise Star-shaped seed pods with distinctive taste, available from Chinese supermarkets.

Tuile A French biscuit, moulded into curved shape while still hot.

Turmeric Spice used in Indian cooking, mainly for its bright yellow colour.

Vanilla pod Fragrant dried pods of the vanilla orchid.

Conversion tables

Temperature

Gas	Electric degrees F	Electric degrees C
1	275	140 very cool
2	300	150 cool
3	325	170 warm
4	350	180 moderate
5	375	190 fairly hot
6	400	200 hot
7	425	220 very hot
8	450	230 very hot
9	475	240 very hot

Weights

1oz	25g
2	50g
3	75g
4	110g
5	150g
6	175g
7	200g
8	225g
9	250g
10	275g
12	350g
1lb	450g
1.5lb	700g
2lb	900g
3lb	1.3kg

Liquids

2fl oz	60ml
3	90ml
5	150ml
10	300ml
15	450ml
1 pint	600ml
1.25	750ml
1.75	1 litre
2	1.2
2.5	1.5